How to
Start My Business

Published by :
Lotus Press Publishers & Distributors

How to Start My Business

Philip J. Samuel

4735/22, Prakash Deep Building
Ansari Road, Darya Ganj,
New Delhi - 110002

Lotus Press : Publishers & Distributors
Unit No. 220, 2nd Floor, 4735/22, Prakash Deep Building,
Ansari Road, Darya Ganj, New Delhi- 110002
Ph.: 41325510, 98118-38000
• E-mail : lotuspress1984@gmail.com
www.lotuspress.co.in

How to Start My Business

ISBN: 81-8382-022-0

Printed & Published by : **Lotus Press Publishers & Distributors,** New Delhi-02

PREFACE

When starting a new business, there are many important decisions to make and many rules and procedures that must be addressed. The number of tasks you need to complete and the information you need to track down before you begin a business can feel beyond overwhelming. Starting a business takes a lot of courage. To be successful—to stay in business—you need more than courage. You need a combination of hard work, skill, perseverance, and good old-fashioned luck.

This book is designed to help prospective business owners with the often overwhelming process of starting a business. It covers a wide range of topics from idea conception, to choosing a business structure, obtaining financing, performing market research, buying equipment, basic accounting, etc. Written in an easy to read format, it includes almost every topic related to starting a business.

Editor

When starting a new business, there are many important decisions to make and many rules and procedures that must be addressed. The number of tasks you need to complete and the information you need to track down before you begin a business can feel beyond overwhelming.

This book is designed to help prospective business owners with the often overwhelming process of starting a business. It covers a wide range of topics from idea conception, to choosing a business structure, obtaining financing, performing market research, buying equipment, basic accounting, etc. Written in an easy to read format, it includes almost every topic related to starting a business.

CONTENTS

1

BASIC NEEDS TO OPEN A NEW BUSINESS

Although your business might have a name, shareholders, and even a lawyer, it won't be worth much to you until you've added some of the final "details" — like customers, suppliers, and employees. For suggestions on how to take care of those last details that are so essential to your business, check out any of the following:

1.1. WHERE TO OPEN YOUR BUSINESS

Deciding where and when to open your new business is often one of the most difficult decisions a business owner faces. These decisions may also be the most important ones because the ultimate success of the business can hinge on where it's located and when it's opened. To work through these decisions, choose one of the following:

1. Choosing whether to lease office space or work from home.
2. Choosing the best geographic location for your business.
3. Negotiating a lease for your office, if that's your decision.
4. Looking at business incubators.

1.2. HOME OFFICE OR LEASED SPACE?

In some cases, your facility needs will be such that you'll have to lease office space. In other cases, your facility needs may be minimal and you can work from home. If you have a choice, and all things are otherwise equal, you should probably work from home, primarily because (1) it's a lot cheaper than renting office space and (2) you have less to lose if your business fails. But your decision probably won't be that easy. The list below identifies some of the questions you should answer, which should help you further explore your choices.

1. Are you disciplined enough to work at home? Can you focus on the work that has to be done or will you be tempted to do other things around the house?
2. Will you be distracted by family and friends if you work at home?
3. Will customers come to your business? If so, will the customers object to coming to your home rather than a business location? Is there sufficient parking available?
4. Will you need employees? Is there adequate space for more than one person to work? Is there sufficient parking available?
5. What are the zoning restrictions, if any, that apply to your home? Are home offices prohibited?
6. Will the home office deduction be available to you? The criteria for this deduction are very specific.
7. Can you afford to lease an office at the outset of your business? Working at home could be much less costly.

For a further exploration of the choice between working from home and leasing office space, see our discussions of businesses that work out well from home and government restrictions on business use of a home.

1.3. SELECTING A LOCATION

An important factor in selecting a location is that you keep a long-term perspective. Site selection can be a big investment. Choosing the right site now can avoid the costs of relocation in the future. Here are some factors that you should consider in making your site decision:

1. Access to public transportation.
2. Availability of inventory and supplies.
3. Availability of utilities.
4. Availability of workforce.
5. Availability of physical plants.
6. Community services and amenities.
7. Cost of physical plant.
8. Location of competitors.
9. Parking facilities.
10. Proximity to markets.
11. Suitability of location for future expansion.
12. Taxes.
13. Traffic flow.
14. Transportation facilities.
15. Transportation rates.
16. Wage scales in the locality.

1.4. LEASING OFFICE SPACE

A lease agreement is a contract between you and the owner of the property. Since it's a legal document, you should have your attorney review it before you sign it.

Lease agreements will vary, so there's no way that you can anticipate every issue that might arise. But all commercial leases should contain certain basic provisions with which you should be familiar.

A lease agreement is generally a long-term commitment for your business. View it as a planning opportunity and keep in mind the following points:

1. Getting out of a lease can be a costly endeavour. Be certain that the location and terms of the lease agreement are right for your business.
2. Being able to obtain additional connected space may be critical for your business in the future. If so, provide for future expansion in your lease agreement.
3. If the real estate market is soft due to an overabundance of commercial lease space or a poor economy, your bargaining power will be greater. In a soft real estate market, you may be able to secure favourable concessions.

1.5. BUSINESS INCUBATORS

A business incubator is a facility that provides economical space, plus business services such as typing and copying, some management advice, and possibly financial assistance. Business incubators are owned and operated by a wide variety of entities and sponsors, including local government, universities, economic development groups, state government and a combination of sources. They're located throughout the country, and there's probably one near you. As their name implies, business incubators are designed to nurture small businesses until they are able to exist on their own. The main benefits are the inexpensive office space and the access to business services.

Private companies are also in the incubation business. Be careful if you're considering one of those companies because they, unlike the non-profit agencies, are in business to make a buck from you. They may try to force you into a long-term lease or other commitment that will hinder the flexibility of your business. Also, their managerial assistance may be useless or nonexistent.

1.6. WHEN TO OPEN YOUR BUSINESS

The simple answer to the question "when?" is: at the point when you've completed all of the steps you need to take in order to set up your business. The important point to remember is that you shouldn't start the business before you're really ready. In some cases, the "when" will be decided for you. In any event, here are some suggestions for timing the start of your business:

1. If your business is seasonal, start it at the beginning of your strongest season.
2. If you intend to start a landscaping business in a cold weather climate, start it at the end of winter or the beginning of spring.
3. If you want to open a retail business, consider starting it just before a holiday shopping season.

1.7. BUYING OR LEASING EQUIPMENT

As a small business owner, you'll probably need some type of equipment, whether it's office furniture, a computer system, or, for some, perhaps even some heavy manufacturing equipment. For any equipment, the process is the same:

1. First, you'll have to determine what you need.
2. Next, you'll have to determine how best to acquire it (for example, whether you should buy or rent).

3. Finally, you'll have to determine how to install it and take care of it.

If you decide to lease your equipment, you'll have to enter into a lease agreement. Since a lease agreement is a legal contract, you should consult with your attorney before signing the agreement. Since equipment lease agreements vary depending on the situation, a list of every issue that could be addressed is not possible. However, you can become familiar with the provisions found in most equipment leases.

1.8. MARKETING YOUR PRODUCT OR SERVICE

How you will market and advertise your product will depend largely on your budget. Those with a large budget might want to consider hiring a marketing consultant to help them. Here are a few suggestions for marketing and advertising:

1. Advertise in the local yellow pages.
2. Mail or hand deliver flyers announcing your business.
3. Ask for referrals.
4. Advertise through coupon mailing services (create coupons for your products or services).
5. Rent customer lists, or better yet, develop customer lists from friends, family, and business associates, and send out direct mailings.
6. Put a business sign on your car door.
7. Get your name out before the public by doing volunteer work in the community.
8. Get your name out before the public as an expert in your field by writing articles or giving speeches to local business groups.

9. Allow customers to sample your product or service by giving it away for free for a short time.
10. Get professionally designed business cards.
11. Put low-cost ads in free community flyers.

1.9. GETTING LICENSES AND PERMITS

There are essentially two types of licenses, general and special. A general business license is assessed annually for the privilege of operating a business in the jurisdiction. A special license is one that is issued to a business that will provide products or services that require regulation. Special licenses are issued to professionals, such as doctors, lawyers and others who have met a certain level of training or education.

Permits: State and local governments regulate the safety, structure, and appearance of the community through the use of local laws, called ordinances. Zoning ordinances, which regulate how property can be use, are a common type of ordinance. Once the jurisdiction determines that you have complied with such ordinances, it will issue a permit that will enable you to operate your business.

If your business is unable or unwilling to comply with an ordinance, you can petition the jurisdiction for a special permit, called a variance, that would allow you to, in effect, violate the ordinance. If you're interested in a variance, talk to your lawyer. Variances are not routinely granted and they can be expensive (in terms of legal fees) to obtain, so make sure you really need the variance before you request it.

Home businesses: If you decide to start a home-based business, one of your first steps should be to find out what your local zoning ordinances allow. Some jurisdictions have zoning ordinances that prohibit home-operated businesses altogether. Most, though, are less restrictive and will prohibit only those businesses that may pose a local health hazard or will disrupt the neighbourhood.

1.10. FINDING CONTRACTORS AND SUPPLIERS

When you start your own business, you may be confronted with the task of finding contractors or suppliers. When searching for good contractors or suppliers, consider taking some or all of the following steps:

1. Talk to local chambers of commerce.
2. Talk to trade associations.
3. Look in the yellow pages.
4. Look in the business-to-business telephone pages.
5. Contact the better business bureau for contractors and suppliers.
6. Contact the small business administration.
7. Talk to friends and business associates.
8. Talk to other small business owners.

1.11. HIRING EMPLOYEES

If you're one of those new small businesses that needs to hire an employee or employees, you have a daunting task ahead of you. The operation of a small business is often such an intimate process that finding just the right employee seems to be crucially important in a way that it often isn't for larger companies. Mistakes in hiring are greatly magnified in a small business.

Not only is hiring an employee an important process, but it can be extraordinarily time-consuming. First, you have to put together an advertisement designed to draw just the right person. Then, you have to weed through the resumes. Then comes the interviewing and then the really hard part — making the final decision. There are some steps you can take to help you get just the right person and to save yourself some time in the process.

1.12. JOINT TRADE ASSOCIATION

A business association can be a valuable resource for your business. Through a trade association, you can make contact with other business owners, keep abreast of current technologies, and possibly obtain other group benefits, such as health insurance. You may also be able to locate contractors or suppliers and may even be able to buy customer lists. If you don't know of any trade associations, ask around. Ask your friends and associates if they know of any trade or business associations. Or contact business owners who are in the same industry as you and ask if they know of any trade associations. You can also call your local chamber of commerce for help.

2

STARTING A NEW BUSINESS

Starting a small business takes a lot of courage. To be successful—to stay in business—you need more than courage. You need a combination of hard work, skill, perseverance, and good old-fashioned luck. Generally, people who start their own business can be grouped into two broad categories. The first group consists of people who know exactly what they want to do and are merely looking for the opportunity or resources to do it. Usually, these people have already developed many of the skills necessary to succeed in their chosen field. They also likely to be familiar with industry customs and practices, which can help during the startup phase of a new business.

The second group consists of people who want to start their own business, but don't have any real definite ideas about what they'd like to do. While these people have developed skills in the course of their employment or education, they may not be interested in opening a business in the same field of endeavour. To evaluate your own aptitude for small business ownership, you need to:

1. Understand the responsibilities of ownership.
2. Set your goals.
3. Find out if you have the right stuff.
4. Estimate the impact on your everyday life.

2.1. OWNERSHIP RESPONSIBILITIES

Probably the two most common reasons that a business doesn't succeed are that 1) the business is poorly managed because the owner lacks the necessary skills and 2) the owner underestimates how much money it will take to start the business. To begin the process of preparing yourself, let's take a look at:

1. Pros and cons of owning a business: Here's where you can get a good sense of the challenges — and the rewards—of owning your own business.
2. Roles you'll be expected to play: How many hats must you wear as a small business owner? Are you ready to be one of Uncle Sam's sales tax collectors? Are you ready to "manage" your customers? Are you ready to be the boss?

As a small business owner, you're going to have less time for your personal life and you'll probably be using much of what you own as collateral to raise money for the business. If you are willing to make those sacrifices, then let's move on to some of the advantages and disadvantages of owning your own business.

2.1.1. Pros of Owning a Business

1. You have the chance to make a lot more money than you can make working for someone else.
2. You'll be your own boss and make the decisions that are crucial to your business' success or failure.
3. You may be the boss of other people.
4. You'll have job security — no one can fire you.
5. You'll have the chance to put your ideas into practice.
6. You may participate in every aspect of running a business.

7. You'll learn more about every aspect of a business and gain experience in a variety of disciplines.
8 You'll have the chance to work directly with your customers.
9. You'll be able to benefit the local economy, such as by hiring other people to work for you.
10. You'll have the personal satisfaction of creating and running a successful business.
11. You'll be able to work in a field or area that you really enjoy.
12. You'll have the chance to build real retirement value.
13. You'll have the chance to put down roots in a community and to provide a sense of belonging and stability for your family.

2.1.1.1. Cons of Owning a Business

1. You may have to take a large financial risk.
2. You will probably have to work long hours and may have fewer opportunities to take vacations.
3. You may end up spending a lot of your time attending to the details of running a business and less time on those things you really enjoy.
4. You may find that your income is not steady and that there are times when you don't have much income coming in at all.
5. You may have to undertake tasks you find unpleasant, such as firing someone or refusing to hire a friend or relative.
6. You may have to learn many new disciplines, such as filing and book-keeping, inventory control, production planning, advertising and promotion, market research, and general management.

2.1.2. Roles Expected to Play

Small business owners are responsible for the entire business, which involves a lot more than just providing goods or services. It's likely that all the administrative and managerial duties currently performed by your employer will fall on you. We've all heard of the beleaguered executive who moans that he's overworked because he has to wear two or three hats at his company. Well, most small business owners would give anything if they had to wear only two or three hats.

Sales taxes and payroll or self-employment taxes will have to be collected and paid. Accounts receivable and accounts payable will arise in almost any business setting. Providing customer service, keeping the appropriate equipment and supplies in stock, as well as tracking and maintaining inventory and work in progress are activities vital to most businesses. As a new small business owner, it's more than likely there'll be no one except you to do them. Here's a look at some of the roles you can expect to play if own your own business:

1. *Tax collector*: If you sell goods at the retail level, you're responsible for collecting a sales tax for various government entities; also, if you have employees, you're responsible for collecting payroll taxes from them.
2. *Manager/boss*: If you have employees, you'll be responsible for all of the human resources-related functions, including recruiting, hiring, firing, and keeping track of all the benefits information; you'll be the one filling out all the insurance forms, answering employee questions and complaints, and making the decisions about whether you should change the benefits package you offer your employees.

3. *Sales/marketing/advertising executive*: In addition to having to plan your marketing or advertising campaign, you'll have to carry it out; you may write advertising copy, do some preliminary market research, visit potential customers, and make sure existing customers stay happy; depending upon the type of business you own, you may have to join business groups, attend various breakfasts, lunches, and dinners, and just generally network with anyone who could help your business prosper.
4. *Accountant*: Even if you have an accountant, you'll have to know a lot about accounting; you'll have to know which records to keep and how to keep them; if you don't have an accountant, you'll also have to prepare all of your tax forms, and you'll have to know how to prepare and interpret all of your own financial statements.
5. *Lawyer*: Even if you have a lawyer, you'll have to know a lot about the law; if you don't have a lawyer, you'll have to prepare all of your own contracts and other documents and understand all of the employment laws if you have employees or want to hire someone.
6. *Business planner*: As you own your business, you'll inevitably want to make changes, perhaps to expand the business or add a new product line; if you want to make a change, it'll be your responsibility to do it; you'll have to plan it and execute it, and you'll have to consider all of the ramifications of your decision.
7. *Bill collector*: When customers don't pay, it'll be up to you to collect from them; you'll have to know what you can and can't do when collecting; you'll have to decide how best to collect from them and when to give up.

8. *Market researcher*: Before you start your business, you'll have to find out who your customers are and where they're located; you may also have to conduct market research at various times during the life of your business, such as when you are considering introducing a new product.
9. *Technology expert*: As a small business owner, you will probably come to depend upon your computer; you'll have to fix it when it breaks, install upgrades, and load software; you'll also have to keep up with the newest products and the latest changes in technology.
10. *Clerk/receptionist/typist/secretary*: Even if you have clerical help, you'll inevitably do some of your filing, some of your typing, some of your mailing, and some of your telephone answering; even if you have someone else, for example, keep track of overdue accounts, you'll have to know how to do it so that you can teach them what to do.

Obviously, much of your time will be spent on the mechanics of complying with the requirements imposed on you as a business owner. If you're going to succeed, you'll have to do so in the time that remains. Don't make the mistake of underestimating the cost, in hours, of being in business for yourself. A person who spends 40 hours a week focused on his or her work will have to work a lot more hours as a business owner to get in 40 hours of activity directly relating to providing customers goods or services. And during the startup period, you'll probably be the busiest you'll ever be.

2.2. GOALS SETTING

For many people, it helps to translate their expectations and desires into concrete terms by setting goals. We've organised these into three broad categories:

2.2.1. Economic Goals

For many entrepreneurs, this is a strong inducement. The opportunity to increase personal earnings and achieve their financial potential is often a powerful motivation in starting a business. Obviously, you want your business to be a success. But how you define success depends on a number of personal factors. Assuming you've been in the work force for a while, you know what kind of lifestyle you can afford on your current income. If you're like most people, you'd probably like to earn more. Many people feel that self-employment is the way to do it. Sometimes, it's economic pressures that cause a person to consider opening a new business:

1. *Increase earnings*: Some people believe working as an employee in a corporate setting limits their earning potential, and they want the chance to make the kind of money they feel they deserve.
2. *Replace earnings*: Some people have been downsized or rightsized, or whatever it's called these days, and they need to replace their lost income.
3. *Supplement earnings*: Changed family circumstances may require a second source of income, which translates into a part-time business.

2.2.2. Personal Goals

Unlike money, many of these factors can't be quantified but are important nevertheless. For many people, the chance to build something of their own, according to their own vision, drives them to start a business. Typical reasons that people choose to start a business include:

1. *Freedom*: Some people just don't like working for others and they want the freedom to make their own decisions. Owning your own business is a way to achieve personal freedom on many levels.

2. *Career change*: Most people change jobs or even careers several times during the course of their lives. Sometimes, it's by choice; other times, existing jobs simply disappear.
3. *Satisfaction*: Some people feel trapped in a field they don't enjoy, and they want a chance to work at something they find more interesting.
4. *Recognition*: Being an expert or authority in a particular field is also an important factor for many people. They don't just want to start a business; they want to be recognised for the quality of their work and their expertise.
5. *Flexibility*: Self-employed people have more freedom to choose businesses allowing them to satisfy personal preferences, such as working outdoors, maintaining hours other than 9 to 5, having seasonal vacations, etc.
6. *Responsibility*: Some feel lost in a corporate setting, and they want the chance to play a bigger role in their chosen field.
7. *Professional growth*: Some people believe their ideas are being ignored or not being used properly in a corporate setting, and they want the chance to do it the "right" way.
8. *Benefits and security*: With corporations looking for ways to control costs, the benefits offered to employees aren't as plentiful as they once were. Many people feel the traditional advantages of working for a large employer are gone. Retirement plans are increasingly less generous, corporate health plans are costing employees more each year, and the job security corporate workers once enjoyed has been greatly reduced.

2.2.3. Retirement Goals

It's vital for everyone, employee and entrepreneur alike, to recognise there'll come a time when you want to kick back and enjoy the fruits of your labour. In this time of growing concern over the continued viability of the Social Security system, any goal-setting you do should involve consideration of your needs after you've built and run your business.

Anyone who has spoken with a personal financial planner knows it takes a lot of money to retire and live comfortably. Many people believe they can do a better job of ensuring they'll have enough money for retirement if they're in charge of the source of their income. In addition, a successful small business can provide more than just steady income saved for the future. Prior to retirement, you may be able to sell your thriving operation for a nice profit. Or you could sell ownership interests to others, who then will run the business while you collect a share of the profits.

Of course, goals won't just determine whether you start a small business, they'll also play a prominent role in just about every decision you make along the way, from how you structure your business planning to whether you hire employees to how you sell and market your product or services.

Short-term Goals: You should also remember that while it's good to have long-term goals, such as getting the business off the ground and helping it grow, you also need to set short-term goals. Your short-term goals should be realistic and achievable. Some short-terms goals might be (1) to select a name for the business that you're happy with, (2) to obtain a business license, (3) to find a good small-business lawyer, or (4) to establish a business credit card account. It'll be important psychologically in those chaotic first months to be able to feel that you're making some progress. Short-term goals can help you achieve those small but crucial victories.

2.3. RIGHT STUFF

There are two distinctly different roles you'll play while preparing to open and run your own small business. Each requires specific skills. On the one hand, you're the person who will be responsible for providing products or services to your customers. This is true whether you have employees or not. On the other hand, you also have to deal with all the activities that relate to running your business. You need to be able to handle both in order to succeed. Since every business is unique, the specific skill set needed to provide products or services will vary. Do your best to gauge the scope of activities that make up the business.

Be particularly careful not to overlook the less-enjoyable aspects of the business. And every business has a few. Regardless of your desire to go into business for yourself, if you lack needed skills, it's unlikely you'll succeed unless you find a way to compensate. To begin the process of examining your strengths and weaknesses, select one of the following:

2.3.1. Strength Assessing

Successful small business owners know their own strengths and weaknesses. They build their businesses around their strengths and they compensate for their weaknesses. If you're to succeed, you'll have to be able to identify what you do well and what you don't do so well. As you evaluate yourself, be honest. You'll only hurt yourself if you're not. Also, don't panic if you discover that you have weaknesses. Every small business owner has them. The key to success is not so much in having every skill as it is in finding ways to compensate for the weaknesses.

2.3.2. Personality Traits of a Successful Owner

To begin the process of examining your strengths, the second step is looking at the personality of owner.

1. *Willingness to sacrifice*: You must be willing to accept the fact that, as a small business owner, you are the last one to be paid. Your bank, your vendors, and your employees are all in line ahead of you and must be paid before you see any of the money. You must also be willing to sacrifice much of what once was your free time to your business. If you like working nine-to-five, knowing how much you'll make, and taking three weeks of vacation every year, don't go into business for yourself.
2. *Strong interpersonal skills*: If you thought that getting along with your boss was tough, wait until you have to deal with suppliers, customers, employees, lawyers, accountants, government officials, and everybody in between. Successful owners are able to work with all personality types, and they're able to find out from their customers what they like and don't like.
3. *Strong leadership skills*: Successful owners understand that others are looking to them to be led to the promised land. Others will be looking to you for answers, and if you're not ready for that responsibility, you probably shouldn't own your own business.
4. *Strong organisational skills:* Successful owners are able to keep track of everything that's going on in their business and they're able to set priorities and get things done. They know that if they lose track of what's going on, they're sunk.

5. *Intelligence*: Successful owners are able to anticipate problems before they arise and to take pre-emptive steps to avoid them, and they know how to solve crises after they occur.
6. *Management ability*: Small business is all about managing relationships, with your customers or clients, with your employees, with your suppliers, with your accountant and lawyer, with your banker, and with your family. If you don't think you can effectively manage those relationships, you shouldn't start a new business.
7. *Business experience*: Without some solid business experience, you're probably not going to be able to borrow any money. Your banker will want to know about your experience, not just in business, but in the same field as the business you're hoping to start. If you lack the experience, go get it any way you can: volunteer at an existing business or try to get a part-time or weekend job in the field.
8. *Optimism*: How will you react when business isn't going as well as you expected? A pessimist may fold the tent, but an optimist who believes in the business will keep going. Successful owners are optimists who are able to weather the rough spots.

2.3.3. Compensating for Weaknesses

At this point, you should have looked at your own strengths and weaknesses and judged for yourself whether you're ready to start a small business. You should also have compared those strengths and weaknesses with the traits you'll need to have if you're to be successful. The next step is to figure out what to do if you don't yet possess all of those traits. If you discover that you don't have all of the traits you need to succeed, don't despair.

Ask yourself if you can pay someone else to perform them. If your list includes items that you can't hire someone else to do, such as working with others, the solution is not so easy. Your best bet may be to partner up with someone whose skill set complements yours. Finding a good partner can be difficult. Most people partner up with those they know best, such as friends and family. But be aware that partnering with those you know best doesn't always work. Some marriages and friendships have been ruined by business partnerships, while others have been enriched by them. Finding a partner through others means, such as through a business association, is even more tenuous. The best advice is to be careful. Make sure that you're a good match before you go into business together.

2.4. ESTIMATING THE IMPACT ON YOUR EVERYDAY LIFE

Being self-employed is fundamentally different than being an employee. The distinction between work time and personal time blurs. If a problem arises with the business, it's *your* problem, and it won't go away merely because you've closed the doors for the day. Decisions you make regarding the business will have a direct and immediate impact on your personal life.

The impact is even greater if your business involves working out of your home. You may experience conflicts over the use of space for business or personal purposes. The distinction between your personal life and business life is even further attenuated. Even when you're at home, you're also physically at work. On the upside, there's no commute and you can eat cheaper at home. If you have a family, it's important to measure the impact opening a new business will have on them. It's best to discuss this as soon as you seriously start to consider the idea. Both you and your family must be willing to put up with the changes in your lives owning a business will bring.

Some people experience emotional and physical strain from being on their own and working the hours it takes to make it. These aspects of day-to-day living will be seriously affected by your decision to open your own business:

1. *Certainty and source of income*: One of the biggest differences between being self-employed and being an employee is the source of your income. Employees can generally expect to receive a paycheck at fixed intervals and for a known amount.
2. As the owner of a new small business, you'll be paid only when and if the business generates enough money. Even successful businesses rarely generate a profit in the beginning stages of operation. You'll have to be prepared for a period during which your expenses will exceed any income derived from the new business.
3. *Health insurance*: Although employees are being called upon to pay an increasingly larger share of health insurance costs, it's even tougher for a small business owner. There is no employer to pick up some portion of the premium cost. There's no pool of employees that would allow you to negotiate a more favourable rate than you can get on an individual policy. On the other hand, you may be able to join an association of other small businesses so you can take advantage of cheaper group insurance rates.
4. *Retirement savings*: Retirement savings are a little different than health insurance. If you don't have health insurance and experience a catastrophic

injury or disease, you may be wiped out. The impact of failing to save for your retirement can be even more damaging, but people tend to minimise the risk because "retirement is such a long way off."

It's no surprise the saving rate is higher among employees than small business owners. Employer-sponsored plans provide a convenient and painless way to set aside a portion of each paycheck. A small business owner has to make a conscious decision to save, outside the framework of a plan administered by someone else. That decision often can be deferred or forgotten when you feel the cash coming in has to be put right back into the business.

3

SETTING UP A BUSINESS ORGANISATION

3.1. CHOOSING PROFESSIONALS

Nearly every small business owner will need the assistance of an accountant, attorney, banker, and insurance agent at one time or another. Some also hire a management or marketing consultant. In fact, if you decide that you do need the help of a professional, finding a good one should be one of the very first steps you take to start your new business. Some of the first steps you'll be taking—deciding on the form of your business. Which professionals will you need? The first step in answering that question is for you to understand how each professional can help you. Types of assistance each can provide to you:

1. *Accountant*: Sets up your books; prepares your taxes; provides you with tax advice related to the operation of your business, such as how to choose the best retirement plan and how to take advantage of tax deductions.
2. *Attorney*: Helps you choose the right form of business; makes sure the proper papers are filed; drafts and interprets contracts and leases; defends you if legal action is brought against your business;

represents you if you bring legal action against someone else; provides you with legal advice related to the operation of your business, such as the rules for hiring and firing of employees.

3. *Banker*: Helps you get financing; helps you establish credit card accounts; works, in many cases, as your silent partner, providing you with business operation advice.
4. *Insurance agent*: Evaluates your insurance needs; provides you with advice on which types of coverage you need.
5. *Management and marketing consultant*: Provides basic business operation advice; provides pricing and inventory advice; provides sales and advertising advice.

An assessment of your business needs does not have to be exhaustive, but it should be as comprehensive as possible. The reason the assessment is necessary is to enable you to make an informed decision about the services the professional will provide. Being aware of the business's needs allows you to consider suggestions from the professional and to make the best decisions for your business.

3.2. BUILDING A BUSINESS PLAN

A business plan is a written document that defines the goals of your business and describes the means you will use to attain those goals. Every small business owner should prepare one, though in reality many do not. Although creating a business plan will take a lot of time, effort, and energy, it'll be well worth the trouble. A business plan can be assembled in any number of ways. However, some essential components should be included in any plan, which are listed in the next page:

1. *Description of the business.* Describe the business, including what the products and services of the business are.
2. *The marketing plan.* Describe the target market for your product and explain how you will reach that market.
3. *The financial management plan.* Detail the costs associated with operating your business and explain how you will pay those costs. Will you need financing to start the business? If so, how much.
4. *The operations management plan.* Describe how you will manage the core processes of your business, including use of human resources.
5. *Those are the basics.* For a complete explanation of how to put together an effective business plan, see our discussion of planning your business.

3.3. ORGANISING YOUR BUSINESS

After deciding that you're going to start your own business, your next step should be to begin planning the most basic organisational aspects of your business — what you're going to call yourself, and whether the business will be a sole proprietorship, partnership, corporation, etc. To begin setting up your business, choose one of the following:

1. Choosing a form of organisation.
2. Naming your business.

3.3.1. Choosing a Organisation Form

Whether you've purchased an existing business or started one from scratch, you must decide which form of organisation is best for your company. The decision can be difficult to make. There are several choices, and each has its advantages and disadvantages. Make sure that you consult with your attorney or accountant before making a final decision. Choose one of the following:

3.3.1.1. Sole Proprietorships

The easiest and least expensive way to begin operating a business is as a sole proprietorship. You simply decide to begin operating the business as a sole proprietor and it's done. There are no documents or forms needed, unless the business will operate under a name other than the owner's name. If the business will operate under a name that is different from the owner's name, most localities will require you to file a fictitious owner affidavit.

A fictitious owner affidavit informs the local government and the public that the business is operating under an assumed name and indicates who the owner is. To find out more about the requirements in your locality, go to or call your local authority.

As the owner of a sole proprietorship, you will be personally liable for all obligations of the business. Personal liability allows creditors of the business to go after your personal assets if the business assets are not sufficient to cover the business debts. Likewise, your personal creditors can go after your business assets to satisfy your personal debts.

Since you will be personally liable for obligations of the business, you should consider whether the business will be exposed to any potential lawsuits.

3.3.1.2. Starting Partnerships

There are basically two types of partnerships:

1. *General partnerships*: A general partnership consists of general partners who share the management of

the entity and are personally responsible for the partnership's obligations.

2. *Limited partnerships*: A limited partnership consists of two classes of partners: general partners and limited partners. The general partners manage the limited partnership and are personally responsible for its obligations. The limited partners are similar to shareholders of a corporation. They cannot participate in the management of the entity, but can only determine who will manage the partnership. The limited partners share in the profits of the partnership, but their losses are limited to the amount of their capital contribution.

3.3.1.3. Limited Liability Companies

A limited liability company (LLC) is a hybrid entity that combines the tax flow-through aspects of a partnership with the liability protection of a corporation or a limited partnership. However, unlike limited partners in a limited partnership, who lose their limited liability status if they attempt to manage the business, a member of an LLC is not prohibited from managing the business. Although the limited liability company form generally results in limited liability for its members, lenders usually require some or all members of a limited liability company to personally guarantee corporate loans.

The LLC is a relatively new type of entity. Since it is so new, the laws among the various states differ somewhat in their treatment of an LLC. As a result, transactions outside the state of formation by the LLC may be treated differently from transactions within the state of formation.

To form an LLC, articles of organisation must be filed with the secretary of state's office. The articles of organisation contain information about the LLC, such as its name, address, purpose, who organised it, who the registered agent is, etc. The operating agreement is similar to a partnership agreement. Its purpose is to guide the conduct of the business. If the operating agreement is not required to be filed with the articles of organisation, it can generally be in written or oral form. As a precautionary measure, the operating agreement should be written to limit future conflicts.

3.3.1.4. Corporations

One of the best-known and most widely used business entity forms is the corporation. Traditionally, corporations are viewed as having four identifying characteristics. The four corporate characteristics are:

1. Continuity of life.
2. Centralisation of management.
3. Limited liability.
4. Free transferability of interests.

The main advantage of a corporation is the liability protection it provides its owners or shareholders. Liability is limited because the corporation is a legal entity that is separate from its shareholder owners. As a separate legal entity, the corporation has a perpetual life.

Also, as a separate legal entity, the corporation is liable for its own debts and can only be held liable to the extent of the corporation's assets. The assets of a shareholder are personal assets that cannot be reached by corporate creditors, unless the "veil" of corporate limited liability is "pierced." The corporate veil is pierced when the required corporate formalities, such as having annual directors' and shareholders' meetings, etc., aren't followed.

In effect, the corporate veil will be pierced when the corporate form is a mere sham that exists to enable shareholders to avoid personal liability. If the veil is pierced, the shareholders will be liable for the obligations of the corporation. Although the corporate form generally results in limited liability, lenders usually require the shareholders of small, closely held corporations to personally guarantee corporate loans. If you personally guarantee the loans, you will have to pay the lender if the corporation is unable to pay.

Forming a corporation is more complicated and more expensive than forming a sole proprietorship or a simple partnership. However, the formation process is not that difficult. To form a corporation, articles of incorporation must be filed with the secretary of state's office in the state in which the corporation is being organised. If the secretary of state's office accepts the articles of incorporation, it will send a certificate of incorporation. Many states require that a copy of the certificate of incorporation be recorded in the local recorder's office where the corporation resides.

A corporation does not have to be organised in the state in which it is going to do business. It can be organised in any state. Many corporations organise to take advantage of favourable corporate laws. However, corporations must register as "foreign" corporations in any states in which they do business, outside of the state in which they were organised. Both organisation and foreign registration entail the payment of initial and annual fees which can add up to substantial amounts of money over time.

Professional corporations. The corporate form can also be used for professional service providers. The main advantage of incorporating is that professionals in the corporation are not liable for the malpractice of others in the corporation, but they still remain liable for their own individual acts. Incorporating a professional corporation is essentially the same as incorporating any other corporation.

A professional corporation however, must identify itself as such by including the following in its name: P.C., P.A., chartered, or incorporated. Once created, only professionals can own shares of the corporation. The corporation can only provide one form of service, i.e., a professional corporation of lawyers who are also accountants can provide legal services but not accounting services. There are many other aspects of professional corporations that should be addressed before you venture into this form of entity. Your attorney or accountant can advise you as to whether the professional corporation is right for your situation.

In general, corporations are separate taxable entities that are subject to federal and state taxation. Corporate income is taxed at the corporate level. When that income is passed on to the shareholders as a distribution or dividend, it is taxed again on the shareholder's individual tax return. Double taxation may be partially or completely avoided in a small business by paying a salary to the employee shareholder. However, the tax laws governing this area are complex and should be discussed with your accountant or your attorney.

3.3.1.5. S Corporations

An S corporation is not a separate type of corporation. An S corporation operates in the same manner as a regular corporation. It must have directors, officers, and shareholders who function in the same manner as their regular corporation counterparts.

The difference between an S corporation and a regular corporation is that the S corporation has elected to be taxed similar to a partnership for federal tax purposes. After making the S election, the income, losses, tax credits, and other tax items of the corporation flow through the corporation to the shareholders. Thus, income is only taxed once, at the shareholder level. If a corporation does not make an S corporation election, corporate income is taxed twice; once at the corporate level, and again at the shareholder level when the corporate income is received by the shareholder as a dividend.

3.4. NAMING YOUR BUSINESS

When selecting a name, try to make the name short, easy to remember, descriptive of the business, and capable of drawing attention. Depending on the business form you choose, you may have to register and/or receive approval from the local or state government where your business is formed. The name of your business must not be misleading or in any way imply something that the business is not. For example, you can't imply that your business is a licensed plumbing contractor if you haven't received a plumbing license. Specific rules and requirements for each of the various business types: sole proprietorships, partnerships, limited liability companies, and corporations.

Sole proprietorships: Sole proprietorships are presumed to operate under their owner's name. If the business will operate under a different name, most jurisdictions require that a fictitious owner affidavit be filed. A fictitious owner affidavit informs the local government and the public that the business is operating under an assumed name and indicates who the owner is. The fictitious owner affidavit usually has to be filed with the district recorder of deeds' office rather than the secretary of state's office.

If you are going to use a name other than your own for your business, contact the county recorder of deeds' office (or government equivalent) that your business will be operating in to get specific information and any necessary forms.

Partnerships: Similar to a sole proprietorship, a partnership is presumed to be operating under the name of its partners. If the partnership is going to operate under a different name, a fictitious owner affidavit is required. A fictitious owner affidavit is usually filed at the county recorder of deeds' office but may have to be filed with the secretary of state's office. A fictitious owner affidavit informs the government and the public that the business is operating under an assumed name and indicates who the owner is.

Limited partnership: Choosing a limited partnership name involves more formalities than choosing a sole proprietorship or partnership name. A limited partnership name has to be reserved with the secretary of state's office. The name is usually reserved when the limited partnership files a certificate of limited partnership with the secretary of state's office to register its existence. The name of the limited partnership must include the words "limited partnership," the letters "L.P." or some other phrase indicating that the entity is a limited partnership.

Corporations: Choosing a name for a corporation is a formal process, just as it is for a limited partnership or a limited liability company. A corporate name has to be registered with the secretary of state's office. The corporate name must be unique and not be in use or reserved for another corporation. If the corporate name you choose is already in use when you file your articles of incorporation, the secretary of state's office will reject your articles of incorporation. You can call the secretary of state's office to find out in advance whether a particular name is available. Or if you have access to certain online services like Lexis/Nexis, a legal research database, you can electronically search your state's database of names to see which names are available.

Most states will allow you to reserve a corporate name for a period of time, provided that the name isn't already in use or already reserved. The name of a corporation must include the words "corporation," "incorporated," "limited" or "company," the letters "Inc.", or "Corp." or some other phrase indicating that the entity is a corporation. Most state statutes specifically identify which descriptions can be used.

S corporations: S corporations are subject to the same name rules that a regular corporation is subject to. An S corporation does not have to indicate its status. An S corporation's status has to be identified when the corporation is filing its income tax return, and, in some instances, when the corporation is filing its state income tax return.

Professional corporations: Professional corporations are generally subject to the same name rules that apply to corporations with one exception. Instead of indicating its corporate status with an "Inc." or other corporate designator, a professional corporation must include the words "professional corporation," the letters "P.C." or some other phrase indicating that the entity is a professional corporation.

3.5. GETTING A LOAN FOR YOUR BUSINESS

New small businesses that need a loan to get started are in a classic catch-22: lenders will want to see a proven track record before they lend you any money, but you can't establish the track record until you get the loan. As a result, a lot of new owners have to turn to alternate sources of financing, such as selling personal assets, borrowing from friends and relatives, or taking on partners or investors.

If the alternate sources of financing are not available to you, don't give up on getting a loan from a bank or other traditional lending source just because you're told that it's difficult to do. If you already have a good credit relationship with a bank, you may have built the track record you need without even realising it. Here are two suggestions for succeeding where others have failed:

Develop a first-rate business plan. If your business plan is well thought out and well put together, you've just improved your chances of getting a loan. Go to banks with a good small business lending record. For a list of the top eight banks in your state, see the best banks for small business.

As part of any effort to raise money for your business, you should develop financial data on your business that you should be prepared to give to a lender. Here's a list of information you should compile:

1. A personal expense budget for one year.
2. A personal financial statement.
3. Estimated startup costs of your business.
4. Estimated first-year business expenses.
5. Estimated total cash requirements.
6. The amount of money you can invest and the amount of money you need to borrow.
7. Estimated break-even point.
8. A business plan.

3.6. SETTING UP YOUR BOOKS

Even if your business has an accountant, you should know something about basic accounting principles. Setting up your books in an organised manner is one of the important, and most ignored, first steps a new owner can take.

4

HOW TO CHOOSE A RIGHT BUSINESS

If you have a strong interest in something, think about the needs of other people who share your interests. Is there something you can provide? It may help to think in terms of goods and services. Most businesses involve a mixture of both, but this dichotomy can help narrow the focus. Ultimately, considering doing something you love is a start, but it has to be further analysed by examining the market potential, competition, resources required to enter the market, consumer/buyer demand, and uniqueness of the idea.

The best place to start in picking a small business is with consumers. Ultimately, whether you succeed will depend upon whether you are able to meet some unmet need in the market. In fact, if you love to cook, you're more likely to succeed if you open an interior decorating service—even if you know nothing about interior decoration — than you are if you open a catering service, if there is a demand for interior decorating services but not for another catering company in your area. It's far easier to hire someone who knows something about interior decoration than it is to sell consumers something that they don't want.

Of course, you don't necessarily have to sell a new or different product or service in order to succeed; you can succeed if you can improve what is already being sold. In the above example, you should open a catering business if you can provide a better service than other catering businesses, such as a wider menu or lower prices. But that's still a function of what consumers want. Your research would have told you that there is a demand for a new catering business if prices were lower or if the menu were more varied. Now that you have an idea of what you need, here's how to get it:

1. A comprehensive study and analysis of all your potential markets is something most small business owners either don't know how to do themselves because they lack the training or can't afford to pay someone else to do because it's so expensive.
2. Once you have some idea of what the market wants, now is the time to begin looking at your skills and experiences. You'll need to match your skills with what the market wants. Once you match your skills to what's available, you should be well on your way to picking the small business that's right for you.
3. A lot of new small businesses fail each year. In most of those cases, the small business owners were probably convinced that their idea for a business was a perfect match for their skills. They were wrong. But you can learn from their errors by avoiding the mistakes they made. In fact, there are some common mistakes that many failed small businesses make.

4.1. TECHNIQUES OF MARKET RESEARCH

If money is not an issue, you may want to contact a market research firm and ask them to analyse your community and find out where small business opportunities exist for you. If, money is an issue, you'll have to gather the information yourself.

A good place to start is with the mainstream press: your newspaper or any of the other business periodicals to which you have access. When you read them, look for trends that may be emerging, not just in business but in our culture at large. To give you some idea of what you should be looking for, here are three examples of current trends and how you might parlay those trends into a small business.

1. *Trend 1*: Increasingly, husband and wife are both wage earners. This means that many couples don't have the time or energy to perform tasks that were most commonly performed by the wife. How can you fill in the gap? Some business ideas are: child care provider, grocery delivery service, house-cleaning service, interior decorator, dog walking service, household manager, and gift purchase and delivery service.
2. *Trend 2*: In an effort to cut costs, many companies have laid off employees. This means that companies are increasingly looking outside of the company to perform tasks previously performed in-house. In business-speak, it's called outsourcing. Ask yourself: which tasks are businesses most commonly outsourcing? Some business ideas are: copywriting services, legal and paralegal services, billing and other human resources-related services, public relations services, and meeting planning.
3. *Trend 3*: Computers are now everywhere. Many businesses, however, lack the in-house expertise they need to take full advantage of the emerging technologies. How can you meet the need? Some business ideas are: Web site developer, graphics

designer, desktop publisher, and database consultant.

In addition to reading newspapers and magazines, you should talk to friends, relatives, business associates, and other small business owners about ideas they may have or needs in the market they don't believe are being met. And, last but not least, don't forget the often most-overlooked resource — yourself. You're a consumer. If you've wished that a particular service were available, chances are that others have too.

When you think about market opportunities, think about how you can improve upon a product or service that is already being provided. But be aware that there are at least two potential stumbling blocks here. The first is the tendency to believe too readily that you can improve upon an existing product or service. This is just old-fashioned overconfidence. Be sure that you've thought through the specific things you can do to improve what's already out there. The second is the fact that your being able to improve upon a product or service is no guarantee of its success. In other words, you must be sure not only that you can improve what's already there, but also that there is also a demand for the improvement. For additional information on how you might develop a market opportunity, consider the following:

Niche Marketing: An approach that is perhaps even more effective than tackling existing businesses head-on is to look for ways that you can perform a service or provide a product that is similar to, but not quite the same as, a service or product already being provided. One example of this approach is to look for a special niche within a given field. To develop a niche, you should be looking for anomalies in the market. An anomaly, in marketing terms, is an unmet need whose time has come to be filled. To support a profitable business, the need must be fairly widespread or growing rapidly. Perhaps one lies hidden in the social and business trends now underway. For example, a lot of couples where both partners work would like hot, delivered, home-cooked meals that vary each night. But no one believes that it's possible.

Additional Social Trends: One great way to find market opportunities for your product or service is to study social and business trends. The challenge for you will be to see if you can find business opportunities in any of these trends:

1. *Baby boomers entering their 60s*—This group has the largest amount of disposable income in history! They're driving growth in many areas, including services, recreation, and general retailing. Consider what that means for opportunities in travel, recreation, vacations, entertainment, food, and clothing.
2. *New boomer crop of children*—While the original boomers had fewer children per household than their parents, their children seem to be having more, thus creating a new crop of boomer grandchildren. Consider what that means for opportunities in child care, toys, and clothing.
3. *Growing disparity between rich and poor*—The middle class is shrinking. Consider what that means for opportunities in home ownership, cars, entertainment, and restaurants.
4. *Increasing globalisation of business*—This should, if anything, continue to accelerate in the coming years. Consider what that means for opportunities in emerging world markets.
5. *Reinvention of religion*—As people continue to cast off traditional beliefs and services, others return to them even more vigorously. Consider what that

means for opportunities in books, tapes, and online services.

6. *Yearning for high-touch products and services*—This includes the nostalgia induced by high-tech solutions to everything. Consider what that means for opportunities in antiques, older homes, home delivery and pickup businesses, and any business owned by friendly service-minded proprietors.
7. *Mass customisation*—This is not an oxymoron but a response to global homogeneity. Consider what that means for opportunities in businesses that provide products or services individually tailored to each customer.

4.2. MATCHING SKILLS TO BUSINESSES

You should begin by listing what you enjoy doing, what your hobbies are, which skills you've acquired, what your work experiences have been, and what your goals are for the business. Although making such a list might seem at first to be a little simplistic, you'll be surprised how much being forced to write down your ideas will help you crystallise what it is you want from a small business.

Compare the list you've just made with your list of what the market wants. Do any obvious matches leap out at you? If not, don't give up. Here are some more tips and suggestions for choosing a new business:

1. Look at the list that you compiled from your market research; eliminate any of the businesses that you don't believe you'll really enjoy owning. As a small business owner, you'll be living, sleeping, and breathing your business - if you don't enjoy that type of business, your chances for success are slim.

2. On the other hand, be wary of relying too heavily on your list of interests when making your choice. Don't forget that most of a small business owner's time is spent on tasks such as managing employees, haggling with suppliers, meeting with your lawyer or accountant, etc.
3. If you don't have a lot of money to start with, look for a business where you get paid up front and you don't have a lot of startup costs.

Look for businesses where you will have a lot of repeat customers or where people will need to keep buying supplies from you. Avoid seasonal businesses. Avoid competing with discounters or with well-established businesses, since it will be just about impossible to compete with their prices. Instead, you'll have to compete in service. Service businesses are the easiest and cheapest to start because you don't have to buy a lot of equipment and you might not need any employees, at least at first.

4.3. COMMON MISTAKES IN CHOOSING A BUSINESS

Although there are many reasons why small businesses fail, one of the most common is in choosing a small business. A lot of people simply make the wrong choice. To help you avoid that error, here's a look at three of the top reasons why wrong choices are made.

1. *Error 1:* Converting a hobby or interest into a small business without first finding out if there is sufficient demand for the product or service to be provided.
2. *Error 2:* Starting the business without adequate planning. Your success is not guaranteed just because you've found a market opportunity that also takes advantage of your skills and experience. There are many other considerations. For example, you still have to figure out if you can raise enough

money to get started and whether you can withstand periods in which little or no revenue is coming in.

3. *Error 3:* Resisting the urge to ask for help. Since you're reading this material, you may have already avoided this pitfall. A lot of people, however, are reluctant to ask others for advice in choosing a business, either because they're too proud or because they don't know that help is available. Help is out there, and, if you shop wisely, it won't cost you an arm and leg to get it.

5

GETTING FINANCE FOR MY BUSINESS

Small businesses usually need more than just cash: they need "smart" money. Smart money means financing that helps your business in the way that you want it to, where the financier provides not only capital, but support and expertise to your business. Smart money could be an SBA guaranteed loan that allows you to keep your ownership interests intact until your business reaches the stage at which you want to sell shares of the business. The problem in locating "smart" money is that the capital market for small businesses is imperfect and consists of a great variety of underpublicised and poorly organised financing sources.

Whether you are trying to locate a bank that is willing to lend money to your small business or whether you are looking for a business "angel" who will contribute needed equity capital, your quest for financing will require that you devote the same attention to obtaining capital as you give to decisions involving the business's basic product or service.

5.1. BUSINESS'S FINANCING PROFILE

Most entrepreneurs consider their resource pool to consist

of whatever personal assets they're willing to sink into the business, and whatever money they might be able to get through a local bank loan. Yet, a number of alternative financing options may be available to you. To assess whether your business can take advantage of any of these financing options, you should begin by realistically evaluating the investment profile and creditworthiness of your enterprise. The basic things to consider are:

1. The stage of your business's development in the financial life cycle of that type of business (e.g., startup, developing, or mature).
2. The appeal of your business and its operators, in the eyes of investors.
3. The amount of capital needed for your business.
4. Whether personal financing can cover most of your needs.
5. Whether insider financing can fill the gap between what you have and what you need.
6. Whether bootstrapping can reduce your need for additional funds.
7. Our quick pick chart showing the best financing options for businesses in different stages of development.

Save Time: Most financiers will request certain financial statements and a business plan from you before they are willing to invest in your business. In order to be prepared for this scrutiny of your business, you should make your assessment of the credit worthiness and investor appeal of your business before you develop a business plan. While the plan should reflect your personal business goals, keep in mind who your audience is, and draft the plan so that it sells your ideas to people who are in the business of making money.

5.1.1. Business Maturity

Where your business is in its financial life cycle — from startup to aging — will often dictate the availability of certain financing alternatives.

1. Startup businesses typically face the greatest obstacles to obtaining financing because they lack a performance record and a credit history.
2. Acquired businesses face fewer obstacles than those being started from scratch, and might have seller financing as an option.
3. Growing businesses generally have more financing options because as a business matures, it establishes credit worthiness and operating success.
4. Aging businesses tend to be cash-rich because new investment is not taking place. Owners are often searching for the best way to sell out.

5.1.2. Startup Small Businesses

Startup businesses often begin with only ideas and enthusiasm. One of the many issues that every entrepreneur must address in starting a small business is the financial reality involved in deciding exactly what he or she wants to do, when it can be done, and how it's going to be done.

New small businesses have trouble securing conventional financing because they present a tremendous risk to lenders and investors. The result is that nearly three-quarters of startup businesses are funded through the owner's own resources, such as personal savings, residential mortgages, or consumer loans. Family members, friends, and investments by private contacts or "angels" provide most of the remaining "seed" funds for new small businesses. You will find that some small business advisors preach that a "survivalist" mentality is the only way to successfully fund a startup business on a shoestring budget.

The most common financial problem for startup businesses is a shortage of short-term cash, and cash flow problems during a potentially long initial period can be fatal to the business. Any debt financing (loans) that the business can secure from traditional lenders, e.g., banks, is likely to be expensive because of the high risks assumed by the financier.

Moreover, unless the business can boast a significant owner investment and marketable collateral, the availability of conventional debt financing is almost nonexistent. This "cash crunch" puts a tremendous focus upon inventory turnover, and the need for immediate revenue often becomes a daily crisis that takes priority over financing for sustained growth or development of new products. Perseverance and a willingness to investigate all sources of financing — from angels to government loan programmes — are invaluable at this stage. The financing pressures of a cash flow shortage has forced many small business owners to take unwise, desperate measures to salvage their business.

5.1.3. Acquired Businesses

In many respects, the financing options available when you purchase an existing business are similar to the options for raising capital in a growing business that you already own. Debt and equity vehicles are typically more available to you than if you were starting a similar business from scratch. Because the target business has a credit history, existing assets, an established operating cycle and business goodwill, lenders and investors can be approached in the same manner as if you were seeking to expand a business you already owned.

The major distinction between financing for the purchase of an existing business and financing to raise funds for your own growing business is that the former offers the opportunity for seller-financing. Entrepreneurs who are selling their small businesses usually realise that they may need to participate in the buyer's financing of the business sale, and they may be willing to negotiate a very favourable debt or equity arrangement with you. Potential advantages to seller-assisted financing include:

1. You may get a reasonable interest rate and a less demanding credit review.
2. The existing assets of the business are often the exclusive collateral for the financing. In contrast to the common practice of conventional lenders, additional or personal assets of the buyer are rarely pledged as additional collateral on a seller-financed loan. Moreover, a seller's valuation of the business's assets (collateral) tends to be higher than that of a conventional lender; a low valuation might appear inconsistent with the asking price for the business.
3. Personal guarantees are less likely.
4. A seller may be willing to take a subordinate (secondary) security interest. The seller may be amenable to taking a subordinate interest to allow you to obtain conventional financing. The incentive for the seller is that the more money you can obtain from other sources, the more money the seller gets upfront. A conventional lender will require a priority claim on business assets and so the only way you may be able to qualify for the loan is to subordinate other creditor claims.
5. The buyer's assumption of the existing debts or liabilities of the business may be a means of reducing the purchase price. Typically, much of the

downpayment or initial cash price of a business sale goes toward a reduction of existing business debt. However, rather than pay off existing creditors, those debts may be assumable by the buyer in exchange for a set-off on the purchase price of the business. The business creditors essentially become financiers for the acquisition.

6. The use of a gradual buyout may be acceptable to the seller. For instance, the business name and goodwill, and perhaps some tangible assets, could be sold upfront; other equipment or property could be leased by the buyer with a optional or mandatory buyout at a future time. The seller may be willing to accept an earnout arrangement, where a portion of the purchase price is depending on the future success of the business.

5.1.4. Growing Businesses

A growing or mature business usually has sufficient stability in its operations so that cash flow problems are not a constant crisis. If the business is successful, internally generated funds from sales and investments can fund many of the business's needs. Typically, growing and mature businesses have more financing options available to them because of their operating history, established value, credit history, and availability of inventory and accounts receivable financing. In addition, the advantages of having established customers and suppliers, efficient internal operating procedures, more sophisticated marketing and advertising, realistic long-term business plans, and the company's emerging goodwill help improve the creditworthiness and investor appeal of the business.

Debt financing becomes increasingly available to a business as its track record supports creditworthiness. If the business has been profitable, debt financing is generally the preferred form of raising new capital for existing businesses. Nonetheless, a growing business may be stifled by inadequate capital for expansion that stems from the reluctance of an entrepreneur to dilute his or her ownership through equity financing.

Sometimes the decision simply comes down to whether you want a profitable, growing business in which you share control or will cash out your interest at a given time, or whether you own a business that fails because you could not raise sufficient capital for the business to grow. Growing businesses can consider raising equity capital through private transfers of ownership interests, by using venture capital firms, or by selling ownership interests through formal limited private offerings or an initial public offering.

Dangers to the financial health of a growing business are often attributable to the business overextending itself or to poor decision-making. If you rush expansion or acquisitions, purchase too many expensive fixed assets, or form unwise associations with other businesses, you may find yourself throwing good money after bad money. Even very "street-wise" entrepreneurs may be better served by engaging professionals to assist in legal and business matters, and by employing experienced management to handle the growing complexities of the daily operations.

5.1.5. Aging Businesses

Many businesses never reach this stage of the business life cycle because they either fail at an earlier stage or they remain healthy, growing entities. An aging business is characterised by a conservative philosophy aimed at maintaining the business's internal bureaucracy and its market *status quo*. Some companies reach the point where innovation and creativity are limited to tinkering with current products and existing markets.

Investment into new product lines and emerging markets represents a financial risk that a complacent ownership is unwilling to assume. Aging businesses tend to be cash-rich because less investment is being undertaken. The financial concerns for owners of aging businesses often involve selling the business and retirement planning .

5.2. NOTHING SELLS LIKE SUCCESS

Every small business owner is convinced that the enterprise will be successful and that investors can be persuaded by these convictions. However, to obtain financing, you will need to provide objective evidence that your business will succeed. On the most basic level, every potential lender or investor evaluates a business by looking at how the injection of cash will be used and how the money will either be repaid or result in a profitable return.

Many of these questions may be answered by data contained in your business's financial statements and projections; however, lenders and investors also make more subjective evaluations of you and your company. These assessments may affect your financing requests even more than the objective numbers. Additional evidence of future success for your business can sometimes take the form of contract commitments from existing or prospective customers, industry or professional opinions, and market research — even if it's informal testimonials.

In your business plan or loan application, make sure to note any advantageous market trends, consumer appeal, management experience, retention of skilled employees, and availability of any special resources, e.g., a valuable patent. Identifying a lender whose strategic approach or special industry focus matches your business will also enhance the subjective appeal of your business.

When you make your case that your business is a worthy investment, keep in mind that most lenders and investors are followers, not leaders, and the best evidence of a good investment will be your prior success in raising capital. A financier wants to spread risk as much as possible, and a certain comfort level may be reached if other investors have a significant vested economic interest in your business. If you can show a strong financial commitment to the business from additional investors, as well as a meaningful personal investment by the business owners, the appeal of your company will correspondingly increase.

Your past business experiences, your expertise, and your managerial skills likewise play a crucial factor in determining the appeal of your business. If you can establish a personal relationship with a particular financier, such as a local community banker, your past successes and business experience are more apt to be considered in determining the likely future success of your business. Use your personal resume, as well as letters of reference from community professionals and business persons, to help project yourself as a reputable, reliable, and creative business person.

5.3. ESTIMATING THE MONEY

Whether you want capital for startup costs, short-term operating costs, or long-term strategic development, you must accurately estimate the amount of money you need. Preparing a realistic projection of the necessary funding will not only force you to consider the wide variety of costs associated with your plans, but also help convince a lender or investor that you understand your business and the relevant market realities.

You can expect a financier to want to know the amount of money you will need from the beginning to the maturity of the project, details on how the money will be used, and most importantly, how the money will either be repaid or result in a profit. All of this information should be included in your business plan and confirmed in your financial projections.

You can make your capital projections appear more realistic by referring to the sales and expense information characteristic of your industry and business that is published in business books, magazines and business columns in newspapers. These compilations can provide you with objective data to support your projections of sales figures and anticipated expenses. When using published sales/expense ratios as a reference for financial projections, choose a business rated in the top quartile of the relevant small business market as a model for sales projections.

The expenses will not necessarily vary with the success of the business and your overall ratio will appear more positive if you've selected a prosperous reference business. You should also be aware that the reasons behind your capital needs may raise some lender concerns about the management and future success of the company. If, for instance, your business is growing, a need for additional working capital may be a result of managerial shortcomings that are causing slow sales, high inventory, slow collections, or unmet short-term debt.

In situations where additional funds are necessary because unanticipated sales volume is creating greater needs for inventory or collection of accounts receivable, management may need to show that the business can expect continued success.

1. If you are estimating the cost of a startup business, additional considerations apply.
2. Whether you are financing a new or existing business, a well-thought-out business plan is essential.

5.3.1. Costs of a Startup Business

Because the costs of a startup business are often underestimated, new entrepreneurs should consider completing, at a minimum, a few basic financial statements even before they attempt to estimate how much money they will need. In addition to a personal financial statement such as the one illustrated above, try preparing the following estimates for initial setup and projected monthly costs.

Initial setup costs: Prepare an itemised estimate of how much it will cost to get your business set up. These will all be pre-opening expenses. Include in your estimate:

1. Purchase/lease and installation of equipment and fixtures.
2. Utility expenses.
3. Advertising.
4. Initial inventory costs.
5. Real estate expenses (or office rental).
6. Professional costs (accounting, legal, etc.).
7. Licenses and fees.
8. Employee expenses.
9. Startup supplies.
10. Insurance.

Prepare an itemised statement identifying both your personal living costs and the anticipated monthly costs of operating the business. Include:

1. Your living costs.
2. Employee wages.
3. Utilities.
4. Advertising.
5. Supplies, inventory, raw materials.
6. Lease or mortgage costs.
7. Insurance.
8. Taxes.
9. Transportation and delivery costs.
10. Any professional costs and any other expenses relating to running the business.

Planning to Succeed: In order to successfully obtain a mortgage, real estate must have three legendary ingredients: location, location, and location. But it also helps if the building looks inviting, has an interesting history, and is surrounded by a few elegant trees. And so it goes with successfully obtaining a business loan: in this case, though, the three key ingredients are planning, planning, and planning — and it also helps if the plan includes some interesting history and a few attractive non-financial facts to round out the package.

Every small business owner is convinced that the enterprise will be successful and that investors can be persuaded by these convictions. However, to obtain financing, you will need to provide objective as well as subjective evidence that your business will succeed — and this evidence should take the form of a business plan.

5.4. PERSONAL FINANCING

Most small startup business are initially funded by the personal assets of the entrepreneur. Some funding for your small business is likely to come from your direct contributions of personal savings or assets to the business. Additional personal funds are often contributed after the entrepreneur borrows money through a personal loan and then contributes that money as an equity investment into the business.

There is a great variety of personal assets that you can use as collateral to obtain cash from a lender, but perhaps the most common source is a residence. You can use this asset to: obtain a first or second mortgage, to refinance an existing mortgage, or to secure a home equity loan or line of credit. The major disadvantage to using your house as collateral is that default on the loan can mean forfeiture of your home. Nearly all commercial banks and residential lending institutions will have options available for home-backed financing.

The period and computation of the rate of interest, upfront points, closing costs, administrative costs and burdens, the length of loan, loan conditions, and default terms all affect the real cost of a loan. Whether or not the local lender will sell your mortgage to another creditor may also be a consideration for you. For second mortgages or lines of credit, you should anticipate that lenders will allow a maximum total mortgage debt, including preexisting mortgages, of approximately 70 percent to 85 percent of the current market value of your residence.

Recently, some lenders have begun offering financing up to 100% of your home's current market value, but interest rates are steep, and the risk of losing your home if your business fails make these loans a last-ditch choice for most budding entrepreneurs. Also, be aware that second, or even third, mortgages will typically have higher interest rates than first mortgages because the lender is subordinate to a prior mortgagor.

Other than your residence, other commonly used collateral for secured consumer loans include other real estate, life insurance policies, any existing machinery or other business equipment, stock, and pension plans. For instance, you can usually borrow the cash surrender value of an ordinary life insurance policy. You are not obligated to repay the loan principal, only to pay interest on the loan. The rate of interest charged depends upon when the policy was purchased; rates on older policies might be very favourable.

Of course, borrowing against your own policy means the eventual death benefit of the policy will be diminished by the amount of the loan, plus the loss of interest. You may also have other assets in your personal portfolio that permit you to borrow from them or that can be used as collateral in a conventional loan. Marketable securities can also be pledged to a bank as collateral for a loan.

5.5. INSIDER FINANCING

After considering their personal resources, the next place most entrepreneurs look for additional financing is to "insiders" like family, friends, or business associates. Borrowing from insiders is attractive because it's private, often informal, usually unsecured, and often includes favourable terms, and because legal default proceedings are seldom invoked.

In addition, this kind of financing can often be incorporated into a family's estate plan to assist in minimising estate and income tax liabilities. However, financing from family and friends is often a double-edged sword. Counterbalancing the convenience and low cost of insider financing are the misunderstandings, personal conflicts, and other problems that can arise from a lack of business formality or economic success. These dangers can seriously damage both the business and the long-term personal relationship between the parties. If you do seek financing from insiders, keep in mind the following suggestions and cautionary notes.

Insider debt financing: If a friend or relative is contributing capital as a gift, you should embody that understanding in a written "statement of gift." The gift may have tax consequences. If the transfer of funds is not intended to be a gift, an enforceable agreement such as a promissory note should be drafted that reflects the nature and terms of the exchange. The temptation to forego arm's-length formalities must be avoided. If the insider does not want to participate in control or ownership of the business, a promissory note stating that the money is a loan, and listing the terms of the loan, should be drafted.

If you want the insider to become an owner of your business in exchange for financing, documentation of the arrangement is again important, but the paperwork will vary according to the type of ownership interest you are transferring. If the business is not incorporated, equity financing should include a drafting or redrafting of the partnership, limited partnership, limited liability operating agreement, or joint venture arrangement. The rights, liabilities, and responsibilities of the new participants should be defined clearly to avoid later confusion, disagreements, or unanticipated liabilities.

5.6. INTERNAL SOURCES OF FUNDS

Bootstrapping is a buzzword that basically means generating needed funds by deftly managing your cash inflows and outflows. Improving cash flow should be a daily task, like housekeeping. Monitoring, forecasting, and analysing cash flows is essential to liquidity and profitability. A basic list of areas of concentration would include:

1. Collection of accounts receivable — Can credit terms or collection procedures be improved? How about billing cycles and/or cash discount incentives?
2. Inventory management — Do you really need all that inventory? It ties up cash, takes up expensive space, ups insurance costs, and often "shrinks" so if you don't absolutely need it for immediate shipping or manufacturing purposes, keep it lean and mean.
3. Accounts payable cycle — Vendors make good financiers. If they offer 30 days to pay, take 30 days and think about asking for 45. Set up a system to take advantage of early payment discounts too.
4. Expense control — Make every dollar count. Do you really need to rent that expensive postage meter or can you just buy self-stick stamps for awhile? Does your company van need to be washed at the fancy place down the block or can you spare a little time to do it yourself on the weekend? Thrift applies to fixed assets, too. Will a used computer do the job you were going to buy that Pentium II for?

A little frugality and sensible use of available resources will pay big dividends in the long run. The old cliche "watch the pennies and the dollars will take care of themselves" is the bootstrapper's fight song.

6

HOW TO KEEP GOOD EMPLOYEES

An organisation is only as good as the quality of its employees. Keeping good help productive and on the job is the keystone of management. It is an everyday, continual process. It represents not one single problem with one single solution but rather a maze of simple and complex problems each with several possible solutions. Successful management deals with each problem and chooses among the alternative solutions. Management is, perhaps, problem solving and decision making. In dealing with problems the manager would do well to keep in mind an old rule "If you are not part of the solution, then you must be part of problem... If you are part of the solution, you are probably part of the next problem."

The problem of high turnover seems more evident in some businesses than in others. The manager who faces this problem should be aware that there is no simple solution, only intelligent choices. In making these choices the manager needs a basic understanding of people and why they do what they do or why they don't do what you would like them to do. The choices management makes in these decisions should be predicated upon the goals of the organisation. The results of such decisions may actually be a test of the validity of organisational goals. Realistic goals which have been developed and accepted by all segments of the organisation will prove to be a much sounder base for management decisions than goals developed from a narrow perspective of any one segment of the organisation. To aid in this understanding, try to take a look at several important processes in human behaviour. These are described below.

6.1. IMPORTANT PROCESSES IN HUMAN BEHAVIOUR

6.1.1. Problem Solving Process

The problem solving process is a sequence of steps which can be utilised in solving most problems. It is an analytical approach which is flexible, adaptable and can be modified to deal with a wide range of problems. There is considerable feeling among management experts that all parties involved in the problem should be allowed to become involved in the solution of the problem. It might also be a wise management decision to allow participation by those who might be affected by the solution. With involvement of this scope, it becomes especially important that a logical process guide be used.

1. *Look at the Facts*: What is presently the situation? Where does it need improvement? What should be left alone? In some management theory "Problem Identification" is cited as step number one.
2. *Identify the Problem*: What specifically is preventing you from reaching a desired performance or level of production? A proper identification of the problem is essential to solve the problem.
3. *State Your Goal in Solving the Problem*: Why do you need to solve the problem and how will you know when the problem is solved? Review alternatives and select one which will most logically help you achieve your goal.

4. *Develop a Plan of Action*: Who will do what; how will it be done; and when will the task be started and completed?
5. *Do It Implement the plan of action*: Check progress toward the goal; make adjustments where needed.
6. *Take a Look at What Has Been Done*: Have you accomplished what you intended? Have new problems been created? What needs to be done next?

6.1.2. Motivation

Motivation is an inward force which causes certain behaviour. Motivation can be either positive or negative. Inward motivation is often a very strong force, often difficult to change and sometimes slow to develop. Long-lasting changes result from inward motivation. Motivation can be influenced by one or several factors. Motivation in job performance may well be influenced by situations which are completely unrelated to the job. The term "lack of motivation" could be more appropriately called "negative motivation."

Because of the very personal nature of motivation, it may be hidden from the eye of the casual observer or disguised by the employee. Motivation is not usually responsive to manipulation. Positive motivation most often arises when the employee feels he is genuinely an important part of the picture or the job. Such feelings usually result from involvement and participation. Strong motivation rises out of a strong feeling of self worth. Management can be most effective by creating an environment which enhances feelings of self worth, involvement, recognition, responsibility, advancement and growth.

Incentive is an outward influence which causes certain behaviour to take place. Incentive is usually thought of in terms of "reward" or "lack of punishment." In many cases incentives can be used to bring about quick changes. The improvements may tend to disappear when the rewards no longer come. Sometimes the level of reward must be continually increased in order to be effective.

6.1.3. Communications

Communication is the keystone to the success of an organisation. Communication is more than writing memos and giving orders. Communication involves more than just talking. Communication is a cycle of activity — sending a message, receiving a message, responding to a message and sending a new message back. Anything less is "non-communication." Within organisations a number of obstacles to communications occur. Some of these obstacles are: ordering someone to do something, threatening or promising certain consequences, preaching or moralising, giving suggestions to influence certain behaviour, criticising, agreeing, name-calling, adversary positioning, consoling and withdrawing from the situation.

A "language gap" may present another common obstacle to organisational communication. A new employee, in particular, may not understand the jargon or technical language of the industry or the company. When company or organisational goals are not in sync with individual goals, we may see a communication breakdown. This may be due to a difference between: 1) What a person sees and/or hears, and 2) What a person wants to see and/or hear.

Communication skills are a package of many different skills. Improving communication skills involves sharpening all these skills.

1. *Listening Skills*: Trying to hear the message as well as hearing the words. Try to find out what the speaker really means. If you understand, say so. If you do not understand, ask for more information or clarification.
2. *Speaking Skills*: Give clear, concise, positive messages. Stress the importance of complete understanding. Express confidence but avoid cockiness. Be alert to signals from your audience.
3. *Read Unspoken Messages*: People often send the unspoken messages through the eyes, the expression, the hands or the feet. Understanding this "Body Language" is a vital element of communication. Actions speak louder than words. Learn to listen to actions and you'll be able to communicate more effectively.
4. *Good News and Then the Bad News*: It is often impractical and impossible to respond positively to every request from every employee. Any manager will, on occasion, have to convey what the employee will view as bad news. In this case, don't pass the buck, stall or avoid the issue. Respond firmly and directly.
5. *Complaints, Criticism and Disapproval*: When an employee is busy at his job or in front of a group of other employees or customers would probably be the wrong time and place to "chew him out." The temper or mood you exhibit will greatly effect the results of the correction offered. Remember, communication is not a one-way street. Employees will respond more favourably to criticisms and suggestions if they know that they, too, have the of opportunity to offer suggestions or respond to criticism. In addition to giving orders and instructions, communications mean caring and

showing appreciation. When management shows appreciation, everybody wins.

Favourable communication probably offers more in the area of job enrichment than any other single factor. Open communication eases tension, reduces confusion, lessens frustration and alleviates boredom — all high factors in job dissatisfaction and high employee turnover. Basically, communications within the organisation should be personal. It's people working with people to accomplish the goal of the organisation.

Keeping good workers at all skill levels is getting more difficult. Employees today will switch jobs more quickly than they did a few years ago. Indeed, workplace loyalty is not what it was. Of course, some employee turnover is inevitable, and sometimes a few "fresh faces" will inject energy and new ideas into a company. Finding qualified new workers is a challenge, but replacing conscientious, dedicated staff is especially difficult, even for firms that can afford to pay above-average salaries. Well-managed companies take measures to keep their good people, and so should yours. Here are a few pointers for keeping your "stars."

Discover the things employees hate and get rid of as many of them as possible. Even ideal jobs have their negatives, and everyone from the CEO to the janitor has to deal with a few aggravations, do tasks they dislike, etc. However, smart bosses always seek to know what irritates and annoys their workers before the irritants and annoyances provoke them to leave the company.

Periodically, ask all employees for their honest opinions, both individually and in groups. Unfortunately, the prospect of getting feedback from the staff scares many bosses, and "gripe sessions" can be unpleasant. However, what you learn can help you resolve long-standing problems and end unpopular practices.

6.2. WAYS TO FIND AND KEEP GOOD EMPLOYEES

There are seven ways to find and keep good employees

1. *Develop a talent mindset*: At all levels of the organisation, that is. You need, across the organisation, a deeply-held belief that having high-caliber people in the most value-creating jobs is critical to achieving the aspirations of the company. To do this you need to develop a rigorous and candid review process to identify high and low performers, outline individuals' strengths and weaknesses, and identify specific actions to address 'under-performers'.
2. *Create extreme Employee Value Propositions (EVPs)*: That deliver on your people's dreams. There are four keys to this mechanism for capturing more than your fair share of talent: a great company, great leaders, great jobs, and attractive compensation.
3. *Build a high-performance culture*: That combines a strong performance ethic with an open and trusting environment. Company culture is a critical element of the EVP. The combination of these two elements – highly competitive and open – is most satisfying for 'talent' to work within.
4. *Recruit talent continuously*: The most aggressive companies are always on the prowl for talent. They have a keen sense of who they are looking for, and they do their looking in new ways and in new places.
5. *Develop people to their full potential*: Every company leaves a tremendous amount of human potential untapped, because its people are inadequately developed. Effectively conceived stretch jobs coupled with informal feedback, coaching and mentoring are enormous developmental levers.

6. *Be ruthless with non-talent*: Act on the negative influence of under-performers. They make you unable to attract top talent, do not develop the people below them, block opportunities for those around them, undermine the morale of the group, and ultimately cause better performers to leave the company.
7. *Re-recruit your top performers*: 'Retention' as a concept is boring. So, think of it as 're-recruiting'. Beyond the EVP, companies must demonstrate that they value and appreciate their people. Simply helping high-potential people feel connected and vital to the future of the business can be a powerful retention tactic.

Following are some tips for attracting and keeping quality people:

1. Develop advertising and marketing programs targeted to potential employees.
2. Use computer-based recruitment tools; ensure your technology is at the same level as that of the labour pool.
3. Network with associations, suppliers, owners, and peers.
4. Establish an internal referral program that pays employees for referrals resulting in a hire.
5. Maintain a visible presence wherever the labour pool frequents, such as industry associations and related events.
6. Have in-house recruitment personnel visit job fairs and colleges, follow up on networking leads, do direct sourcing, and surf the Internet.
7. Use a specialty recruitment firm to supplement your internal hiring efforts.
8. Recruit retirees and minority workers.

9. Use the Government Employment Exchange as a resource.
10. Help the construction industry enhance its image as a career for today's youth.

6.2.1. Attracting and Keeping Your Future

There are three key ingredients to effective employee recruitment and retention:

1. Identifying why employees leave,
2. Appreciating employees financially, and
3. Creating a better working environment.

Determine why employees leave: When a problem arises on the job site, everything comes to a halt until the problem is identified and corrected. Rarely do contractors follow the same process when an employee leaves. If they did, they just might find reduced turnover. Of course, contractors don't have to wait until an employee leaves to begin taking preventative measures.

Many of the underlying reasons employees leave are similar and, surprisingly, have little to do with money. Often, they leave because of a human factor such as conflict with management personnel, broken promises, or perceived lack of appreciation, support, or direction. Other reasons have nothing to do with the employer at all, such as a need to be geographically closer to their families. Whatever the reasons, employers need to understand them and work to minimise their effects in the future.

Appreciate employees financially:

1. *Pay market wages*: Accessing market information on compensation averages has never been easier. Associations, recruitment firms, even the Internet make compensation surveys readily available. Any

employee worth keeping is smart enough to monitor these figures to make sure he is getting paid fair market value.

2. *Offer stock plans*: The most loyal employee is the one with ownership in the firm. Lawyers and architects have been offering their key people partnerships and shares in the company for decades.
3. *Supplement with bonuses and performance-based pay*: Many firms offer their employees bonus plans—distributed over three and five years—that take into account personal performance, team performance (or project performance), and firm profitability. Payment on commission has been common on the sales end for years. But the industry is now seeing more operations staff earning the bulk of their compensation through bonuses and/or commissions.
4. *Improve benefits*: Perks to a compensation program don't have to cost a great deal of money. And the message they send to the employee can mean increased loyalty and reduced turnover. Many perks now focus on helping the worker succeed both as an employee and an individual. Common incentives include tuition reimbursement for qualified programs, retirement plans, child-care subsidies, and flexible schedules to attract working parents.
5. *Offer employment contracts*: Employment contracts are considered standard procedure for key hires. However, they are becoming popular for retaining existing employees. Contracts are being used to forge employee partnerships or alliances with the employer to reduce turnover.

6. *Improve the working environment:* Most people spend more time with their co-workers than with their families. In fact, for many workers, the workplace functions as a surrogate family—with the worker looking for support, encouragement, and appreciation. The extent to which employers provide this type of atmosphere can be a good determinate of how successful they are in reducing turnover. Here are some nonfinancial tools contractors are using to help boost retention rates:
   a. *A career plan*: Employees like to have clearly defined goals, as well as defined plans and schedules to achieve those goals. Help employees develop a career plan within the firm so they understand where they are going and why it makes sense to achieve those goals.
   b. *Open dialogue*: Sharing of operating and financial information helps build trust between employer and employee. It also helps workers understand how their performance affects results and encourages input. This ultimately invests them with a feeling of ownership in the company and a long-term stake in its future.
   c. *Listen*: One of the most valuable tools a manager has is the ability to provide regular feedback. Keep suggestion boxes for company improvement available to all employees and offer rewards for the suggestion of the week or month.
   d. *Team building*: Provide reward and recognition programs that recognise performance and achievement. Hold regular company social outings to build rapport and enthusiasm.

The wide availability of similar technologies and the growing consolidation of vendors are quickly leveling the playing field for most companies. As competition within the construction industry continues to grow, success will be judged less on price and quality of work and more on the company's ability to provide responsive and informed service. All this points to the critical importance of attracting and maintaining a well-trained and loyal workforce.

The first companies to realise that their success hinges on serving their customers will also be the first to realise that, to maintain that level of service for the customers, they must first provide it internally to their own people. In that respect, a firm's first and most important customer may wind up being itself.

7

HOW TO LEAD AND MOTIVE

A leader is interpreted as someone who sets direction in an effort and influences people to follow that direction. How they set that direction and influence people depends on a variety of factors that we'll consider later on below. To really comprehend the 'territory' of leadership, you should briefly scan some of the major theories, notice various styles of leadership and review some of the suggested traits and characteristics that leaders should have.

7.1. LEADERSHIP

There are also numerous theories about leadership, or about carrying out the role of leader, e.g., servant leader, democratic leader, principle-centered leader, group-man theory, great-man theory, traits theory, visionary leader, total leader, situational leader, etc.

7.1.1. Styles of Leadership

Leaders carry out their roles in a wide variety of styles, e.g., autocratic, democratic, participatory, laissez-faire, etc. Often, the leadership style depends on the situation, including the life cycle of the organisation. The role of leadership in management is largely determined by the organisational culture of the company. It has been argued that managers' beliefs, values and assumptions are of critical importance to the overall style of leadership that they adopt. There are several different leadership styles that can be identified within each of the following Management techniques. Each technique has its own set of good and not-so-good characteristics, and each uses leadership in a different way.

7.1.1.1. Autocrat

The autocratic leader dominates team-members, using unilateralism to achieve a singular objective. This approach to leadership generally results in passive resistance from team-members and requires continual pressure and direction from the leader in order to get things done. Generally, an authoritarian approach is not a good way to get the best performance from a team. There are, however, some instances where an autocratic style of leadership may not be inappropriate.

Some situations may call for urgent action, and in these cases an autocratic style of leadership may be best. In addition, most people are familiar with autocratic leadership and therefore have less trouble adopting that style. Furthermore, in some situations, subordinates may actually prefer an autocratic style.

7.1.1.2. Laissez-Faire Manager

The Laissez-Faire manager exercises little control over his group, leaving them to sort out their roles and tackle their work, without participating in this process himself. In general, this approach leaves the team floundering with little direction or motivation. Again, there are situations where the Laissez-Faire approach can be effective. The Laissez-Faire technique is usually only appropriate when leading a team of highly motivated and skilled people, who have produced excellent work in the past. Once a leader has established that his team is confident, capable and motivated, it is often best to step back and let them get on with the task, since interfering can generate resentment and detract from their effectiveness. By handing over ownership, a leader can empower his group to achieve their goals.

7.1.1.3. Democrat

The democratic leader makes decisions by consulting his team, whilst still maintaining control of the group. The democratic leader allows his team to decide how the task will be tackled and who will perform which task. The democratic leader can be seen in two lights: A good democratic leader encourages participation and delegates wisely, but never loses sight of the fact that he bears the crucial responsibility of leadership.

He values group discussion and input from his team and can be seen as drawing from a pool of his team members' strong points in order to obtain the best performance from his team. He motivates his team by empowering them to direct themselves, and guides them with a loose reign. However, the democrat can also be seen as being so unsure of himself and his relationship with his subordinates that everything is a matter for group discussion and decision. Clearly, this type of "leader" is not really leading at all.

7.1.1.4. Self-Leadership

If we ever hope to be effective leaders of others, we must first be effective leaders of ourselves. To better understand the process of self-leadership and how we can improve our capability in this area, we should first explore the meaning of the word "leadership.

Perhaps the most useful definition of leadership is simply "a process of influence." This short definition is actually quite broad and meaningful. It recognises not only the importance of human influence in the determination of what we are and what we do, but also the complex nature of leadership. The existing literature on leadership is almost universally focused on influence exercised by one or more persons over others. In taking an initial step toward understanding and improving our own self-leadership, we must first recognise that leadership is not just an outward process; we can and do lead ourselves.

Self-leadership in practice:

1. Self-leadership has been more broadly defined as "the process" of influencing oneself to establish the self-direction and self-motivation needed to perform.
2. Research across a variety of settings, from the educational domain to the airline industry, has shown that the practice of effective self-leadership by employees can lead to a plethora of benefits including improved job satisfaction, self-efficacy, and mental performance.
3. Self-leadership involves "leading oneself" via the utilisation of both behavioural and mental techniques. Behavioural self-leadership techniques involve self-observation, self-goal-setting, management of antecedents to behaviour, modification of consequents to behaviour (e.g., self-reinforcement, self-punishment), and the finding of natural rewards in tasks performed. Mental self-leadership techniques involve examination and alteration of self-dialogue, beliefs and assumptions, mental imagery, and thought patterns. Effective self-leadership is not founded on narcissistic or

"blindly" independent employee behaviours with total disregard to the work group or organisation. Rather, effective self-leadership involves a coordinated effort between the employee and the group and/or organisation as a whole.

4. Implicit in this view is a potential trade-off or balance between the self-leadership of an individual employee and the self-leadership of the work group and/or organisation as a collective. This suggests that effective self-leadership involves achieving an equilibrium between focusing on the cohesiveness of a work group and/or organisation and focusing on the value and identity of each individual employee.

Thus, self-leadership does not require entirely autonomous behaviour without regard to the team or organisation. Nor does it require that the identity and value of each individual employee be entirely put aside in favour of the work group or organisation. Rather, an effective self-leadership perspective would encourage individuals to find their own personal identity and mode of contribution as part of establishment of a group or organisation that produces synergistic performance.

Self-leadership provides considerable promise for taking the pursuit of employee effectiveness to the next level. Indeed, effectively self-led employees, both behaviourally and cognitively, may offer the best blueprint for achieving employee and organisational effectiveness in the 21st century.

Leading and Motivating of Employees: Leading and motivating yourself is one thing, leading others is something else. The different styles and kinds of leadership:

1. *Dictatorship*: Striking fear into the hearts and minds of employees never results in positive production.

Usually you will produce a work force that are afraid to make suggestions or grow their positions by accepting more responsibility. If you have employees handling dangerous materials you may need to be a dictator about their respect of safety regulations for their own protection.

2. *Democratic Leadership*: Can you always be fair to everyone? This often fails in government and may also fail in your business. If you are managing a group or team with many diverse personalities, you may need to be more democratic in your leadership.
3. *Leadership by example*: Better, but don't expect clones of you. Each person brings their own skills and traits to the job. They will get the job done, but not the same way you would. The best use of this style is to show a positive example not a negative. If you have strict company policies that everyone, from the top down, must follow you will set the example for others by following them to the letter.
4. *Silent or Low-Key Leadership*: This type of leadership is often mistaken for lack of leadership. You must communicate with your people. There are certain employees, over time, that need little or no supervision. Communicate when necessary but use low-key leadership. Don't rock the boat if it's sailing smoothly.

7.2. MOTIVATION

If you want to motivate a person positively, find out what they are interested in. What is their one overpowering burning desire? It may not be money. Some people just want to be appreciated for their efforts. Get to know your employees on a personal level. Support them and help them achieve their goals and they will move mountains.

Encourage them to measure their efforts and teach them how to improve performance as a way of obtaining their personal goals.

If you suspect that you may have a problem with low morale because employees are exhibiting symptoms of it or because a survey that you've done of your employees indicates it, you need to determine which aspects of your workplace are creating the dissatisfaction with the job and then remedy them. There are several good ways to increase morale and motivation without incurring high costs. Whether your employees are disgruntled or not, you should check out these strategies to see how you can make their work lives more satisfying and productive:

7.2.1. Building Employees' Involvement

Every employer's dream is to have employees who care as deeply for the success of the business as they would if the business were their own. While you may never get employees to care *that* much, you can build a sense that what's good for the business is good for them. Here are some steps to building that type of commitment and involvement:

1. *Identify any problems that might stand in the way.* Again, the types of problems that lead to absenteeism, turnover, and generally low morale will be barriers to developing the type of commitment to the business that you're seeking.
2. *Share your vision and the mission of the business.* As the leader, you need to have some goals for the business. If your goal is to have the best reputation for customer service, for example, employees know what to strive for and have a goal. Getting them involved creates ownership of the business's vision. If employees understand why the goal is important,

they will feel personally responsible for making it a success.

3. *Give some power to employees.* If you want employees to care, you have to give them some responsibility and some decision-making latitude. Employees have to believe that the decisions they make and the work they perform has a direct impact on the product or service you provide. This may be easier to achieve and demonstrate in a small business than it would be in a larger one.
4. *Encourage risk-taking.* Let employees experiment and try to find new ways to help the business reach its goals. Don't create a culture where employees are afraid to try anything new because if they fail they will be punished. Allow a certain amount of failure, and reward people for trying.
5. *Use reward systems.* When your employees do well, reward them. Tailor your reward systems to specific accomplishments. If you have one employee who sells 25 percent more than everyone else, but everyone gets the same bonus, your star sales rep. isn't going to be particularly motivated to excel in the future.
6. *Plan social and athletic activities.* These types of activities allow people to interact with each other on a level that can build stronger professional bonds. If your business is small, perhaps just an annual dinner or picnic somewhere is enough. If you have several employees with a similar hobby or athletic interest, maybe your business can sponsor a team in a local league.

7.2.2. Building Employees' Self-Esteem

Many people believe that work performance is a reflection of how employees feel about themselves and their work. If an employee is proud of the job that he or she does, the work quality will reflect that. Employees who have bad self-images are more likely to exhibit those negative feelings in their work. There are an infinite number of ways, depending on the employee and the means at your disposal. Some ways are as simple as recognition; a simple thank you or a reward for a job well done. This can be particularly gratifying for an employee with a behind-the-scenes job. Other ways to help build employee self-esteem are:

1. Sponsor employees in weight control or fitness programmes.
2. Pay for employees to attend public speaking or other professional development classes.
3. Pay for employees to learn about personal financial planning, either through classes or literature.
4. Ask employees to teach you and other employees a skill or procedure that they do well.
5. Recognise successes, both personal and professional, such as an employee completing her graduate degree or an employee earning his black belt in martial arts.

7.2.3. Recognising and Rewarding Employees

Everybody likes to have his or her achievements recognised by others. Even though personal satisfaction will come from meeting a predetermined goal, it is always more meaningful if someone else is there to share the success. Workers are usually not averse to putting out an extra effort when the business needs help in overcoming a problem or meeting a production deadline. But if the extra effort goes unnoticed, employees will wonder why they should bother.

A moment or two from you to thank the employee and emphasise how that employee's efforts have helped will cost nothing and will go a long way toward increasing the employee's self-esteem and motivation. In devising your recognition and reward programme, consider:

There are no hard and fast rules about when or what types of occasions merit special recognition. Some of the more common reasons for recognition and reward are:

1. Length of service.
2. Retirement.
3. Safety.
4. Attendance.
5. Productivity.
6. Customer service.
7. Superior performance awards.
8. Employee-of-the-month programmes.

What rewards can you give? Typical rewards given in conjunction with employee recognition are:

1. Certificates.
2. Plaques.
3. Trophies or ribbons.
4. Jewelry (pins, pendants).
5. Pens or desk accessories.
6. Watches and clocks.
7. Cash bonuses.
8. Savings bonds.
9. Tickets to sporting or cultural events.
10. Vacation trips.

Here are some other more inexpensive forms of recognition are the following:

1. *Write personal notes to employees.* Jot down a message to one of your employees, recognising him or her for better performance on the job, or write a thank you note to an employee for putting in extra time in the workplace. Use your personal stationery.
2. *Create a "year in review" booklet.* Have a year-in-review booklet with pictures or a celebration highlighting your employees' proudest achievements of the year.
3. *Give courtesy time off.* Grant employees an afternoon off, or even a day or two of leave for special, personal events in their lives.
4. *Give credit when credit is due.* Remember to give credit to those who have introduced great ideas and completed special projects.
5. *Put up a bulletin board.* Construct a bulletin board at your place of business to recognise employees through letters, memos, pictures, thank you cards, and other methods.
6. *Have a "Friday surprise."* Surprise your staff with something nice on Friday, recognising them for working hard or just hanging in there.
7. *Get a travelling trophy.* Establish a trophy that goes each month to the employee exhibiting the greatest overall performance — behaviours and results — in the business.

How to reward and recognise: How you present your reward and recognition is almost as important as what you recognise and, arguably, more important than what you give as a reward. If in giving the best reward you can afford for a special occasion you simply drop the award off on the employee's desk while mumbling a "thank you" on the way out the door, you've wasted your money and may even have done more harm than good. Recognition that means anything is given with sincerity and thoughtfulness. It must be treated as special, because that's what it is. It should *not* be treated as some necessary evil. If it's worth doing, it's worth doing right. Recognising an employee is not an end in and of itself. It's a means to an end — making the employee feel valued and reinforcing desirable behaviour.

Generally if something is worth recognising, it is worth publicising. Unless you have an employee who is extremely shy and introverted, a little celebration is a good way to bestow recognition, whether it takes the form of a plaque, a bonus, a certificate, or just some words of praise and a "thank you." Some suggested ways to bestow recognition are:

1. Bring donuts and coffee, and make the presentation during the morning coffee break.
2. Set aside some time at a regularly scheduled meeting to recognise achievements.
3. For more formal presentations, have a dinner.

If the employee is shy and likely to feel uncomfortable, you may choose to send an e-mail message or a memo publicising the achievements of the employee instead of having an in-person gathering.

8

HOW TO GET EXPOSURE FOR MY BUSINESS

Someone is talking about your product or service to someone else and that person has the ear of a major publication or electronic media. In other cases the business person took a chance and contacted the media with a press release at the right time with the right message. Sometimes the exposure can be negative. Consumer Reports found and ranked your product dead last in a comparison test. Are you ready for the negative as well as the positive?

The best place to start is with yourself. Is there something about your product or service that is "newsworthy?" If there is, the best place to take that information is to your own industry. Almost any industry you can name will have some kind of association tied to it. These associations will have trade magazines, journals or at the very least, a newsletter.

If you are fortunate enough to be featured in media, don't forget to let the local media know about it. Small towns love it when locals make the "big time." Also be sure to let employees know about your exposure. It will add to their self-esteem that they are working with a company with national or international recognition. Don't forget important contacts of your business. We have more confidence when we think we are dealing with a major player. It's OK to blow your own horn about your success.

There may come a time in your business when you need to hire a Public Relation (PR) firm. This usually happens because something negative is happening in your business. Lack of sales or some other catastrophe has sent business into a downward spiral. The PR firms job is to pull you out. In the event that this happens, make sure you arm the PR people with everything they need to do the job. Don't hold back any negatives about the company. Sooner or later the media will discover the negatives and you will find yourself in worse shape than before.

Public Relations is a business of persistence. Keep sending the information out. If you really have a worthwhile product or service, someone will eventually see it and you're on your way.

8.1. ATTRACT MEDIA EXPOSURE FOR YOUR BUSINESS

You have built a good business, you have a story to tell and you want to attract more customers. Unfortunately, not enough people have heard of your company. Getting news coverage in the press is an important part of any sales and marketing strategy. For better or worse, opinions are formed by what people see and hear in print, radio and television. Good press can help the selling of your products and services. After you do get coverage, the reprinted piece can be used in your marketing material for added credibility.

The last thing a reporter wants to report on is a thinly disguised promotion for your product. Instead, they will often refer you to their advertising department where this type of promotion belongs. By positioning a top-level executive within your company as an authoritative expert who is able to provide the media with bigger-picture content. Most PR people agree that if you can help the journalist as a resource, you will eventually get publicity and simultaneously establish your company as a leading industry expert and authority in the field. This will typically lead to profitable things for your company.

Getting media attention for your company is not a one-shot time but rather an all-the-time thing. Be patient. It takes time.

8.2. EXPOSURE THROUGH ADVERTISING AND PROMOTIONS

Advertising and promotions is bringing a service to the attention of potential and current customers. Advertising and promotions are best carried out by implementing an advertising and promotions plan. The goals of the plan should depend very much on the overall goals and strategies of the organization, and the results of the marketing analysis, including the positioning statement.

The plan usually includes what target markets you want to reach, what features and benefits you want to convey to them, how you will convey it to them, who is responsible to carry the various activities in the plan and how much money is budgeted for this effort. Successful advertising depends very much on knowing the preferred methods and styles of communications of the target markets that you want to reach with your ads. A media plan and calendar can be very useful, which specifies what advertising methods are used and when.

For each service, carefully consider: What target markets are you trying to reach with your ads? What would you like them to think and perceive about your products? How can you get them to think and perceive that? What communications media do they see or prefer the most? Consider TV, radio, newsletters, classifieds, displays/signs, posters, word of mouth, press releases, direct mail, special events, brochures, neighbourhood newsletters, etc. What media is most practical for you to use in terms of access and affordability? You can often find out a lot about your customers preferences just by conducting some basic market research methods.

Immediate response advertising is designed to cause the potential customer to buy a particular product from you within a short time. Advertising results should be checked daily. Since most advertising has some carry-over effect, it is also a good idea to check advertising runs two weeks after, three weeks after, and so on, to ensure that no opportunity for using profit-making messages is lost.

Attitude advertising is the type you use to keep your store's name and merchandise before the public. Some people think of this type as "image building" advertising. With it, you remind people week after week about your regular merchandise or services or tell them about new or special services or policies. Such advertising should create in the minds of your customers the attitude you want them to have about your store, its merchandise, its services, and its policies. To some degree, all advertising should be attitude advertising. It is your reputation builder.

Attitude (or image-building) advertising is harder to measure than immediate response advertising because you cannot always attribute a specific sale to it. Its sales are usually created long after the ad has appeared. However, you should keep in mind that there is a lead-time relationship in such advertising. In short, 'attitude advertising' messages linger in the minds of those who have had some contact with the ad. Sooner or later, these messages may be acted upon by people when they decide to make a certain purchase.

Because the purpose of attitude advertising is spread out over an extended period of time, the measurement of results can be more leisurely. Some attitude advertising — such as a series of ads about the brands which the store carries — can be measured at the end of one month from the appearance of the ads or at the end of a campaign.

8.2.1. Planning For Results

Certain things are basic to planning advertisements whose results can be measured. First of all, advertise products or services that have merit in themselves. Unless a product or service is good, few customers will make repeat purchases no matter how much advertising the store does. Many people will not make an initial purchase of a shoddy item because of doubt or unfavourable word-of-mouth publicity. The ad that successfully sells inferior merchandise usually loses customers in the long run.

Small marketers, as a rule, should treat their messages seriously. Humour is risky as well as difficult to write. Be on the safe side and tell people the facts about your merchandise and services. Another basic element in planning advertisements is to know exactly what you wish a particular ad to accomplish. In an immediate response ad, you want customers to come in and buy a certain item or items in the next several days. In attitude advertising, you decide what attitude you are trying to create and plan each individual ad to that end.

1. *Plan the ad around one idea.* Each ad should have a single message. If the message needs reinforcing with other ideas, keep them in the background. If you have several important things to say, use a different ad for each one and run the ads on succeeding days or weeks.
2. *Identify your store fully and clearly.* Make sure your radio and television ads identify your sponsorship

as fully and frequently as possible without interfering with the message. Logotypes and signatures in visual ads should be clean-lined, uncluttered, and prominently displayed. Give your address and telephone number. It's possible to use a musical or sound effect signature identified with your store to create a "logo" on radio too.

3. *Pick illustrations which are similar in character.* Graphics - that is, drawings, photos, borders, and layouts - that are similar in character help people to recognize your advertising immediately.
4. *Pick one audio format or type face and stick to it.* Using the same type face or the same audio format for radio or television helps people to recognize your ads quickly. Using the same format or kind of type and illustrations also allows you to concentrate on the message when checking ad response changes.
5. *Make copy easy to understand.* Printed messages should be broken up with white space to allow the reader to see the lines quickly. Broadcast messages should be written conversationally.
6. *Use coupons for direct mail advertising response as often as possible.* Coupons give an immediate sales check. Key the coupon in some manner so that you can measure the response easily. In your radio ads, you can have listeners create their own "coupons". One fast food chain asked listeners to hand draw a coupon and bring it in for a free hamburger.

In weighing the results of your immediate response advertisements the following devices should be helpful:

1. *Coupons brought in*: Usually these coupons represent sales of the product. When the coupons represent requests of additional information or contact with a salesperson, were enough leads obtained to pay for

the ad? If the coupon is dated, you can determine the number of returns for the first, second, and third weeks.

2. *Requests by phone or letter referring to the ad*: A "hidden offer" can cause people to call or write. For example, in the middle of an ad include a statement that on request the product or additional information will be supplied. Results should be checked over a one week through six months or 12 months period because this type ad may have considerable carry-over effect.
3. *Testing ads*: Prepare two ads and run them on the same day. Identify the ads — in the message or with a coded coupon — so you can tell them apart. Ask customers to bring in the coupon or to use a special phrase. Run two broadcast ads at different times or on different stations on the same day with different 'discount phrases'. Ask a newspaper to give you a 'split run' — that is to print "ad 'A'" in part of its press run and "ad 'B'" in the rest of the run. Count the responses to each ad.
4. *Sales made of a particular item*: If the ad is on a bargain or limited-time offer, you can consider that sales at the end of one week, two weeks, three weeks, and four weeks came from the ad. You may need to judge how many sales came from in-store display and personal selling.
5. *Check store traffic*: An important function of advertising is to build store traffic which results in purchases of items that are not advertised. Pilot studies show, for example, that many customers who are brought to the store by an ad for a blouse also bought a handbag. Some bought the bag in addition to the blouse, others instead of the blouse. You may be able to use a local college or high

school distributive education class to check store traffic. Class members could interview customers as they leave the store to determine which advertised items they bought, what other items they bought and what they shopped for but did not buy.

8.2.2. Use of Different Media

When your ads appear simultaneously in different media — such as the newspaper, on radio and television, in direct mail pieces, and as leaflets — you should try to evaluate the relative effectiveness of each. You can check one printed medium against the other by using companion (the same or almost identical) ads in the newspaper, direct mail, and leaflets.

You can make the job of analysing and comparing results from among the media easier by varying your copy — the message. Your ad copy, thus, becomes the means of identifying your ad response. You can check broadcast media — radio and television — by slanting your message. Suppose, for example, that you advertise an item at 20 percent reduction. Your radio or television ad might say something like this: "Come in and tell us you want this product at 20 percent off." You can compare these responses with results from your "20 percent off" newspaper ad. Require the customer to bring in the newspaper ad — or a coupon from it.

Some of the ways to vary the copy are: a combination of the brand name with a word or some words indicating the product type; tone of voice; speed of delivery; picture variations; size variations; and colour variations. Check your printed ads against each other as well as against your radio and television ads.

Even one ad, commercial or highway poster can result in sales for one product and attention for your business. You should remember, however, that a series of ads that are related will result in sales over a longer period of time than the campaign lasts. Your business name will become very much better known. Your expenditures for advertising therefore, should be scheduled over a period of three, six and 12 months. Avoid deciding to advertise this week and putting off the decision about when you will next advertise.

9

USING INTERNET FOR MY BUSINESS

9.1. BUSINESS NETWORKING ON THE INTERNET

The internet is a vast store of information and data, some of which could be highly valuable to you. But finding the specific information you need can be difficult and time-consuming. Among the millions of interconnected sites that make up the World Wide Web, there are many that can save business people time and money. You can source information and contacts for any aspect of your work.

The web is growing daily. Some sites may close, others will change. A website lets you put your products in front of a worldwide audience. It can help you generate new revenue, cut costs and build better relationships with both customers and suppliers. The costs of setting up a website are relatively low, so every business should think about having one.

You can design your website yourself, using modern software that makes it no harder than using your familiar word processing software. You can hire a web design agency to do it for you. Or you can use a service that gives you a fixed-price deal for a set number of pages.

9.1.1. Marketing on the Internet

Using the internet gives you access to a number of powerful marketing techniques. The Internet can improve the reach and cost-effectiveness of your marketing. It can help you build your company's reputation and win new customers.

9.1.1.1. Trading on the Internet

The Internet enables you to sell 24 hours a day to customers anywhere in the world and the sales process can be fully automated. Your Internet shop can attract new customers and provide better service for existing customers. The increasing availability of low-cost broadband connections and increasing consumer confidence in online security means the number of people shopping online is growing rapidly. It is now possible to buy and sell just about anything on the Internet.

9.1.2. Intranets

Intranets is a tool for better business. An intranet is like your own private Internet. It uses the same technology as the World Wide Web and the same easy point-and-click approach. An intranet does not have to be large. It might just link three people working for the same business in three different locations. An intranet can give you better access to information, better co-ordination of people and resources, better customer handling and more cost effective ways of working. It may also provide you with internal e-mail facilities.

Simply using a computer to hold and process business information creates a security risk. Connecting the system to the Internet increases the threats to which it is exposed and the potential damage from a security breach.

Networking is one of the most effective ways to find clients for any consulting or professional services business. But if you limit your networking to only what you can do in person, you'll be missing out on a huge number of possibilities. Networking is more than entering a room full of people and exchanging business cards. It's creating a pool of contacts with whom you can exchange clients, referrals, resources, ideas, and information. Networking can happen by phone, by mail, over coffee, and increasingly, over the Internet.

The growth of the Internet has created many new ways to network without ever leaving your home or office. Pick a topic, any topic, and there will be multiple web sites and online communities devoted to it. Almost any type of Internet presence offers opportunities for networking.

10

MINIMISING RISK IN MY BUSINESS

Most people believe it is best to stick one toe in to test the waters first, and most new businesses start on a part-time basis, while the owner is still working elsewhere. To find out ways to reduce your risk and to learn what to do when a business isn't a success, consider the following:

10.1. HIRING FAMILY MEMBERS

Family-operated businesses make a lot of sense in certain instances. You must always look at more than just the dollar decisions when involving family. The majority of new small businesses involve the owner's family in some way. This involvement may range from having the spouse do the bookkeeping to having the children work part time after school. Getting help from family members can be a great, not to mention inexpensive, way to help you get through the startup phase of your new business. Family members can also help alleviate the additional time and frustration requirements of your new business.

Another consideration is how it will affect nonfamily employees, if you have any. When it is time to promote an employee, will it automatically be the family member? These decisions will affect all of your employee-employer relations with the other employees. On the positive side, a family member will be more willing to step into your shoes when needed. For example, if you get tied up doing something, a family member usually makes a reliable fill-in.

10.2. FRANCHISING

A good way to reduce your risk of failure is to purchase a franchise because franchises typically have a higher success rate than other types of small businesses. Conventional wisdom holds that franchises have a failure rate of about 5 percent, compared to the 50 percent failure rate of independent entrepreneurs. Successful franchisors have developed "formulas" for starting a new business. The good franchisors want your new business to succeed. If you fail, they fail.

Normally, when you purchase a franchise, you must follow guidelines on what you have to do as a franchisee. These guidelines will decrease your new business startup errors. The franchisor will provide you with guidelines on site specifications, the maximum that you should pay for your location, and other useful information. The franchisor will also provide you with lists of equipment and fixture requirements for your new business, which might keep you from purchasing too much equipment.

An experienced franchisor with a long track record will be able to provide you with the failure rate of the specific business. This will give you a much clearer idea of your chances for success when making the decision to start a new business. On the negative side, a franchised operation will typically be more expensive than other types of startups. Also, some franchises will require you to purchase supplies and various items through the franchisor that may cost you more.

10.3. HIRING A MANAGER

If you're uncertain about your ability to run a small business, one good way to offset that concern is to hire someone to run the business for you. This accomplishes two purposes. First, the manager can bring instant experience to the new business. Second, if you have another job, you'll be able to continue with your current employment, and you'll have something to fall back on if your new business fails. But a few words of caution about hiring a manager.

First, your new business will be only as good as your new manager. If you by chance hire a bad manager, your new business may never recover from it. Second, hiring a new manager can be expensive, especially if you want one with experience in the field. Just make sure that the benefits outweigh the costs. Third, there really isn't such a thing as a part-time small business. Even if you hire a competent manager, you'll be amazed at how much time your small business will demand of you. So be prepared to work long hours in addition to those you put in on your other job.

10.4. USING A HOME OFFICE

Operating a small business from your home is a nice, cost-saving alternative for some people. If a home office makes sense for you, this option will reduce the risk and cost of starting a new business in many cases. You can save on rent and other costs associated with opening a business outside the home. In some instances, home office startup costs will be next to nothing, thus minimising your financial risk in starting the new business.

If your new business is not a success, the shut-down costs should be minimal. For example, if you were renting outside space on a five-year lease, you would be potentially responsible for five years of lease payments even after your business shut down.

10.5. STARTING PART TIME

For those who are unsure about whether they can make a go of a new business, starting out on a part-time basis is a viable alternative. A part-time business will reduce your new financial risk significantly while you gain the experience you need. And, of course, if the business fails, you can fall back on your full-time job. An example of a part-time business is doing paid work for friends or family on the weekends or in your spare time. Others choose to start with only a single client or customer and use vacation time to provide the service.

Going into a part-time new business will also enable you to get the kinks worked out of your new business before operating on a full-time basis. Remember that a part-time business will usually not generate a large profit. In some instances, a person may be able to live off of a part-time business, but this is not usually the case. You should also remember that there is really no such thing as a part-time small business. You'll be surprised how much time a "part-time" business will take, even if you have only one client or customer. If you decide to work part-time, be prepared to work long hours

If you feel that you lack business experience and you're not sure that you're capable of running even a part-time small business, get the experience any way you can. If you have to, volunteer your services or work for next to nothing at a business that's similar to the one you want to own. Just because you consider your new business part-time, the related costs of doing business do not necessarily go down.

Suppose you're planning to open a home-based business. The office will require a complete separate set of office equipment. If your business is part-time, that means only that you are willing to generate income on a part-time basis; it doesn't mean that your office expenses will be smaller. A desk and chair cost the same if you sit in it for 10 hours a day or two hours a day.

10.6. KNOW WHEN TO CUT YOUR LOSSES

If you don't decide the financial commitment to your new business in advance, you may regret it in the future. For example, suppose you have Rs. 2,500,000 in cash and investments that you have accumulated from past saving. You're going to open a new business that you're willing to limit to a Rs. 500,000 cash commitment of your own money. The business is losing money and needs additional funding. What will you do? Will you increase your cash commitment or will you consider it time to cut your losses? If your business has lost the Rs. 500,000 commitment, stop at that amount.

10.6.1. Save Money

Make sure you've made the appropriate changes to your new business to make it a successful operation. Don't just presume the business will get better. How long are you willing to commit to an operation that will barely support itself? Would your time be better spent starting another new business that is related to your current idea or would you be better off becoming an employee for someone else? Before you start your new business, it would be a good idea if you also have time commitment goals as well.

The following are different ways to cut your losses if your business is failing or has failed. Some options will work better than others, but just remember that there is no ideal way to get out of a failing business.

1. *Sale of the business*: A voluntary sale of your business may be the least painful way to get out of your business. A voluntary sale usually will allow you to sell your business for the most amount of money. Most potential buyers are willing to spend more on a business that is still in operation and has some ongoing business value.
2. *Forced liquidation of the business*: This occurs when the creditors force the sale of company assets. This can be an expensive option because the price received may be substantially less than you would get in a voluntary sale of the business. In some instances, it may make sense to sell parts of the business and to wait until you find the best buyer for each business part.

10.7. FINANCING ASSESSMENT

Finding the money needed to start a new business is almost always one of the most difficult hurdles new owners face. At this point in the process of analysing your business idea, you should have examined both the costs of starting a business and your market with the result that you know how much it should cost and how much you should be able to earn.

Assuming that the startup costs are more than you have on hand and more than you'll be able to earn right out of the gate, the next step is to figure out whether you can raise the difference. Commercial lenders tend to shy away from new small businesses because they believe the risks of failure are too high. Commercial lenders want to see a history of success and a solid credit record. Thus, a lot of small businesses that need to borrow funds to get started find themselves in a classic catch-22: the bank won't lend them money unless they have a solid track record but they can't build the record until they get the money.

One possible solution is to look to smaller lenders with good reputations for small business lending. Bank mergers and consolidations have forced some of the smaller banks to take some chances they perhaps wouldn't have taken before. Small businesses are often the beneficiaries of those changes.

10.8. LEGAL ASSESSMENT

In making a legal assessment of your business idea, you need to determine to what extent the operation of your business might expose you to legal liability. Talk to your lawyer and ask him or her about the risks. Once you determine the risks, there are, of course, steps that you can take to protect yourself. One way is by purchasing insurance. Another way to protect yourself is by incorporating your business so that the risks would be borne by the company and not by you. But corporations may not be for everyone because they can be expensive to create and a lot of trouble to maintain.

SUGGESTED READINGS

Abrams, Rhonda M. (1993). *The Successful Business Plan: Secrets & Strategies.* Oasis Press.

Antonini, Orlando J. (1993). *Getting a Business Loan.* Crisp Publications.

Bangs, David H. Jr. (1990). *The Market Planning Guide.* Upstart Publishing Co.

Baumbach, Clifford M. and Kenneth Lawyer. 1989. *How to Organize and Operate a Small Business.* Prentice Hall, Inc.

Berle, Gustav. (1993). *Retiring to Your Own Business.* Puma Publishing Co.

Cook, M. (1992). *Big Business: How to Launch Your Home Business and Make it a Success.* Collier Books.

Dahle, R. (1983). "So You Want To Start A Business." North Carolina Agricultural Extension Service.

Davis, Dale A. (1991). *How to Develop and Market Creative Business Ideas.* Oasis Press/PSI Research.

Eyler, David R. (1991). *Starting & Operating a Home Based Business.* John Wiley and Sons, Inc.

Hevron, John. *Business Success: A Guide to a Proper Beginning.* Hevron and Hevron.

Joseph, Nekoranec & Steffens. (1992). *How to Buy a Business.* Enterprise-Dearborn.

Kahn, Sharon and the Phillip Lief Group. (1988). *101 Best Businesses to Start.* Doubleday.

Kamoroff, Bernard. (1992) *Small-Time Operator: How to Start Your Own Small Business, Keep Your Books, Pay Your Taxes, and Stay Out of Trouble*! Bell Springs Publishing, Laytonville.

Kishel, Gregory & Patricia. (1994). *Growing Your Own Business.* The Berkley Publishing Group.

Knight, Brian and the Associates of Country. *Buy the Right Business—At the Right Price.* Upstart Publishing.

Lane, Byron. 1990. *Managing People—A Practical Guide.* Oasis Press.

Makus, L.D. et al. (1993). "Planning Your Business." *Cooperative Extension System.* University of Idaho. CIS 978.

Martin, Charles L. (1988). *Starting Your New Business—A Guide for Entrepreneurs.* Crisp Publications, Inc.

McGregor, Ronald J. (1993). *Buying a Business: Tips for the First Time Buyer.* Crisp Publications.

University of Nebraska (ed.). (1996). *Setting Up Your Own Business: Financing Your Business.* Cooperative Extension. NebFact.

Whitmyer, Claude and Salli Rasberry. (1989). *Running a One Person Business.* Ten Speed Press.